THE LITTLE BOOK OF INDIAN BUSINESS

THE LITTLE BOOK OF INDIAN BUSINESS

Short, Sharp, Supersmart

FINSHOTS

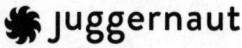

JUGGERNAUT BOOKS
C-I-128, First Floor, Sangam Vihar,
Near Holi Chowk, New Delhi 110080, India

First published by Juggernaut Books 2024

Copyright © Finshots 2024

10 9 8 7 6 5 4 3 2 1

P-ISBN: 9789353459154
E-ISBN: 9789353453787

All rights reserved. No part of this publication may be reproduced, transmitted, or stored in a retrieval system in any form or by any means without the written permission of the publisher.

Typeset in Adobe Caslon Pro by
R. Ajith Kumar, Noida

Printed at Thomson Press India Ltd

CONTENTS

Preface ix

ECONOMY AND PUBLIC POLICY

Is this India's decade?	3
Is India getting rid of poverty?	11
What is the lifecycle of a currency note?	18
How will India's demographic dividend pan out?	19
Why do the rich keep getting richer?	26
Should we have a four-day workweek?	32
How does the RBI control inflation?	39
What is the impact of the third gender on the economy?	47
Were the 1991 economic reforms genius – yes or no?	52
What is e₹ (e-Rupee)?	60
How does government control inflation?	66

Should India print more currency if we need more money?	69
How do interest rates impact our economy?	74
What if we abolished the Income Tax?	75
What is inheritance tax? Is it a good idea?	80
What is the impact of long notice periods?	87
What if women were paid for daily chores?	93
Where did India's missing monuments go?	100
Why does India have a pension problem?	107
How is the Union Budget of India prepared?	114
How does the RBI make money?	118
What is the value of a tree?	123

CAPITAL MARKETS

What is Modern Portfolio Theory?	129
What is the Buffett Indicator? Is it foolproof?	135
What's the dark underbelly of the stock market?	143
Why are TV news stock recommendations a sham?	153
Why do people really buy the dip?	160

How can you be a rational investor?	166
Which state has the highest number of investors?	182
What is CAGR?	184
What is P/E RATIO?	185
What is EBITDA?	186
What is call option?	187
What is put option?	188
What are forwards and futures?	189
What is blue chip stock?	190
What is VIX?	191
What are growth stocks and value stocks?	192
What is upper and lower circuit?	193

BUSINESS

What are tax havens and why do they exist?	197
What are the brands that have helped build India?	204
What is the price of your attention?	210
Why are CEOs overpaid and employees underpaid?	215

How did businesses forge ahead after Partition?	219
The biggest crypto scam in history?	228
Why are Indian malls dying?	236
Do ATMs need a pay rise?	242
References	249
About Finshots	274

PREFACE

Five years ago, in an IIM Ahmedabad dorm room, the seed of what would later become Finshots was planted. If you had asked us then if we would ever write a book, we would have scoffed at you. We were aspirational but didn't dare to dream that big then. Today, despite all odds, you are reading a compilation of some of our best work – you are holding a Finshots book!

When we started the Finshots newsletter in 2019, our goal was very simple – change the way India's youth thinks about finance and economy. Make it accessible, easy to understand, interesting and free of confusing jargon.

Over the years, we've tried to do just that – one story at a time. Thankfully, our readers noticed what we were doing differently. And they have been our biggest champions and supporters. In fact, when we set out to create Ditto Insurance – our insurance advisory platform – with the same no hidden charges, no spam and 100% honest information ethos – our readers showed their support once again, making us one of India's biggest and most loved insurance distributors.

While they appreciate all our work with both Finshots and Ditto, they've been writing countless emails and comments to make one consistent request:

'Why don't you publish a book, Finshots?'

'Make a paperback already, Finshots!'

'Why not put this all into a book?'

So, we finally had to listen.

The Little Book of Indian Business is our attempt to make reading about business, finance and the economy enjoyable. Complete with some of our best explainers and infographics, this book is aimed at answering some of the questions you may (or may not) have thought about.

This book has been a labour of love and we hope you enjoy reading it as much as we've enjoyed writing it.

And if you've been with us from the beginning – a big thank you from the bottom of our hearts. We owe it all to you. If you've only just discovered us – welcome to our community.

Happy reading!

Bhanu Harish Gurram
CEO, Finshots and Ditto Insurance

ECONOMY AND PUBLIC POLICY

IS THIS INDIA'S DECADE?

India has emerged as the fastest growing economy in the world. We're a bright spot in a world that's struggling to deal with inflation and faltering growth. And Borge Brende, the President of the World Economic Forum (WEF), thinks India's position will only get better. In fact, he likened India's growth trajectory to the snowball effect.

What's that, you may ask?

Well, it's not an obscure economic theory. Rather, it's an analogy that can be pretty much applied to everything. Imagine a snowball that's rolling down a big slope. It might start off small but keeps picking up snow along the way, getting bigger and bigger. It has momentum on its side and grows exponentially. Now imagine this happening to an economy. As the production of goods and services, investments and disposable incomes rise, the economy grows and gathers momentum. There's no stopping this snowball!

And it's not just Brende who thinks this is India's time to shine. McKinsey's CEO Bob Sternfels believes it's not just India's decade, but India's century. Morgan Stanley estimates that we'll become the third-largest economy by 2027.

So, what does everyone think is driving the snowball effect in India, you ask?

For starters, there's India's large population. Nearly 70% of the population falls in the working age group of 15–64 years. And the outcome of this is that there will be fewer 'dependent' people in the country as a proportion of this working-age population. This also means that we'll have a larger part of the population who can spend and drive consumption growth in the economy. Also, with the proliferation of nuclear families, and the children of these families migrating to big cities for work, it could also spur urban consumption. You could see demand for housing and vehicles increase too.

Then there's the government's focus on spending money on infrastructure. As Chris Wood, who writes the Greed & Fear report for Jefferies, said:

'One obvious point here is the transformation of physical infrastructure, where the fiscal deficit has in recent years been primarily spent on investing in infrastructure and not on entitlements. The result is that the huge deficiencies in infrastructure, so visible when Greed & Fear first visited the country on a business trip back in 1996, have now been largely addressed.'

Of course, that's anecdotal evidence. But the hard numbers speak for themselves – we're actually spending more on things that can have a multiplier effect, by generating more jobs. We used to spend just 0.3% of our GDP on roads and railways, now that's up to over 1.5%. That's a figure that *The Economist* called 'eye-watering' because it's around twice of what America and most of Europe are spending on infrastructure.

The end result is projects such as the dedicated freight rail corridors which, for instance, can cut the time taken for transporting goods from Delhi to Mumbai by 50%.

But the government is not just building infrastructure for the sake of it. You see, quite often, you might have noticed a new road being paved. Then, a few weeks later, you'd see the road being dug up to lay pipelines. And a few months after, you may see a few folks digging it up again, maybe to lay telecom cables. That certainly is a waste of resources.

Now that's just an example at the micro level. But similar things can happen in the process of building large-scale infrastructure, too. So, the government has launched programmes, such as the PM Gati Shakti National Master Plan for Multi-modal Connectivity, which aims to get different departments to coordinate with each other, so that capital is resourcefully used and inefficiencies are reduced.

And in the midst of all this, the socialist roots are being catered to as well – not by extensive reliance on subsidies, which investors always place a red flag on, but by improving the distribution of welfare subsidies. You see, back in 2012, the then Finance Minister Pranab Mukherjee had said, 'I lose my sleep not when I look at the volume of quantum of subsidy, but because it is not reaching to the poor and needy and targeted group.' Well, the situation is better now, because leakages are being plugged with the help of Aadhaar card and the Direct Benefit Transfer. Together, they help identify the beneficiaries and the money is deposited directly into their bank accounts. And apparently, we've saved $27 billion this way by preventing leaks in the system.

This can help uplift those who need subsidies the most, and who in turn could even contribute further to India's consumption story.

And what do you think happens when companies around the world notice these changes?

They ramp up their investments too. Slowly but surely, they start announcing and building new projects. For instance, new project announcements from private companies in India have jumped from ₹5 lakh crores in FY21 to a massive ₹26 lakh crores in FY23. Foreign companies, like Apple, decided to set up manufacturing units here instead of in China.

That's the snowball effect kicking in.

Now remember, this isn't a comprehensive list of everything that contributes to the snowball effect, just some of the more visible ones. There are other parameters as well, such as how the electrification of the 600,000 villages in India and the increase in broadband connections (from 61 million to 816 million), will give a boost to productivity. But we'll stop at that.

And this brings us to the final question – what about the hurdles in this plan?

Well, a young population is not a guarantee of rising consumption. For that to happen, we will need to generate high-quality jobs, too. And that has been something of a struggle for the country. The International Labour Organization (ILO) says that the unemployment rate for those with either a bachelor's degree or higher is a staggering 29% in India.

And even though we're spending on infrastructure, we might need more. A whole lot more. In fact, the government thinks we need to splurge at least $1.5 trillion in this next decade. But the problem is that all that money might just be needed to make up deficits – or whatever we failed to build and upgrade in the past. It may not necessarily drive big growth.

There's also the matter that despite everyone talking about this being India's moment, foreign direct investments (FDI) have dropped by nearly 22% in FY23 compared to the previous year. And even though private investments from companies are being announced, we need to see how it translates into ground reality. The government also doesn't think it's enough. In the past, too, they had asked companies to pull up their socks and double-down on their investments.

And finally, our growth is driven by domestic consumption, a trend that cannot go on forever. Since a large part of the economy is still heavily dependent on agriculture for livelihoods, climate change and issues such as heat and water stress could dampen rural incomes, which in turn will affect domestic consumption.

So yeah, while we have a lot going for us, there are some battles we need to fight. Let's keep our fingers crossed.

IS INDIA GETTING RID OF POVERTY?

248 million.

That's how many people we've pulled out of poverty since 2005–2006, as per the National Institution for Transforming India (NITI) Aayog.

But wait … when you hear poverty, you're likely to think of it in monetary terms. If you know that it requires ₹x to lead a basic life – with access to food, clothing and shelter – you can perhaps assess that if someone has succeeded in earning more than that, they have crossed the poverty threshold.

And it's an idea that has been prevalent for over 200 years. Yup, the first real measure probably dates back to 1795 in the UK. A priest named David Davies decided to evaluate the lives of labourers in his region. To that end, he calculated how much money people would need to live in 'tolerable comfort'. And he came to the conclusion that anything below that would make them poor.

So yeah, we're kind of used to having a standalone measure to determine poverty. It's fairly easy.

But that's not what the NITI Aayog measured. They took a more holistic approach and looked into something called Multidimensional Poverty.

What's that, you ask?

Well, think about what outcome you get when using a number to measure poverty. You simply get to know who's poor. And you realize that these are a set of people who are unable to eke out a decent standard of living.

But it doesn't tell you 'how they are poor', that is, the aspects they lack in.

For instance, back in the day, we arrived at a monetary value by first looking at how many calories a person needs daily. We concluded that

2,400 kilocalories in rural and 2,100 kilocalories in urban areas would determine the poverty line. Then we'd look at the wholesale price of certain food commodities and then say a person needs ₹x to buy the food needed to fulfil the required intake of kilocalories. But the problem with this calculation is that one can meet the calorie count even by consuming stuff like sugar, since the method doesn't consider a person's nutrition intake.

So, a person might be earning enough money, signifying that they're above the poverty line, but they're nutritionally poor.

And it's not just about nutrition, of course. That's one example. It could be about children getting appropriate schooling, receiving a steady supply of electricity, having access to clean drinking water or simply having access to bank accounts to receive government benefits that might be directly transferred to them.

Because being deprived of these elements creates a situation where poverty becomes a never-ending cycle, compounding a family's hardships.

And Multidimensional Poverty Index (MPI) seeks to measure just this. It takes into account numerous variables – health, education, standard of living – which present a more holistic picture of where things might be going wrong. And this helps governments refocus their efforts, too. If they know that malnutrition is a major problem, they can launch a scheme where fortified grains are included in the public distribution system. Similarly, if the metric indicates that people in the villages are deprived of electricity, the priority could be to ensure the electrification of all villages.

Anyway, MPI is important because, quite often, things might be even more dire on this front than what simple monetary metrics indicate. For instance, the World Bank pointed out that globally 9% of people lived in monetary poverty in 2018. But if you included all these other variables (health, education) and then measured multidimensional poverty, the number jumped to 14.5%.

So yeah, that's what the NITI Aayog's *Multidimensional Poverty in India Since*

2005-06 paper tells us too. They measured multidimensional poverty and concluded that 248 million people in India have escaped the clutches of multidimensional poverty, and that the prevalence of such poverty is falling dramatically.

Sounds good, no? It's definitely something to cheer about.

But, not everyone agrees with using Multidimensional Poverty Index (MPI) as an indicator to gauge poverty, and there have been some quibbles about the NITI Aayog paper. For instance, some might argue that people are getting access to government benefits, and the subsidies for foodgrains and cooking gas could be helping them. That they may still not be earning the money required to keep them afloat. That if one day, suddenly, the tap on the benefits is turned off due to financial difficulties at the national level, the problems will be exacerbated.

But until then, as economist Ajit Ranade says, 'If some lack of purchasing power is compensated by welfare spending and direct benefit transfers, then that should be counted as income for the recipient.'

It helps.

Next, as Santosh Mehrotra, a professor of development economics, highlights, there could be the problem of projections.

For instance, consider the year-on-year change in the twelve indicators – nutrition, child and adolescent mortality, maternal health, years of schooling, school attendance, housing, household assets, cooking fuel, sanitation, drinking water, electricity and bank accounts – for MPI. The government compared improvements or deficiencies recorded in the National Family Health Survey (NFHS) between 2005–06 and 2015–16. For years where data might be missing (2014 for instance), they assumed a linear growth rate to calculate a drop in poverty. And then, they took the survey data for 2019–2021 and simply extended the gains into 2022 and 2023. It's a simple projection, and the actual data may not back up the calculations.

But even then, there's no denying that the poverty rate has fallen.

A 2023 report published by the United

Nations Development Programme (UNDP) uses similar survey data in India to discuss the state of poverty. It doesn't interpolate or extrapolate the data, and notes that in 2005–2006, 55% of India's population lived in multidimensional poverty. This halved to 27% by 2015–16, and further fell to 16% during 2019–2021.

So yeah, despite all the criticism, we definitely seem to be doing some good work on alleviating such poverty. And that is cause for cheer.

WHAT IS THE LIFECYCLE OF A CURRENCY NOTE?

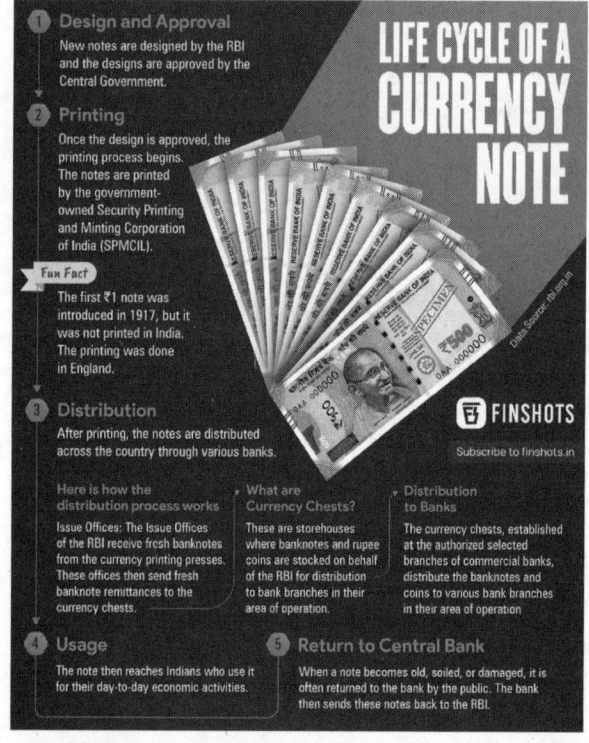

LIFE CYCLE OF A CURRENCY NOTE

1. Design and Approval
New notes are designed by the RBI and the designs are approved by the Central Government.

2. Printing
Once the design is approved, the printing process begins. The notes are printed by the government-owned Security Printing and Minting Corporation of India (SPMCIL).

Fun Fact
The first ₹1 note was introduced in 1917, but it was not printed in India. The printing was done in England.

3. Distribution
After printing, the notes are distributed across the country through various banks.

Here is how the distribution process works
Issue Offices: The Issue Offices of the RBI receive fresh banknotes from the currency printing presses. These offices then send fresh banknote remittances to the currency chests.

What are Currency Chests?
These are storehouses where banknotes and rupee coins are stocked on behalf of the RBI for distribution to bank branches in their area of operation.

Distribution to Banks
The currency chests, established at the authorized selected branches of commercial banks, distribute the banknotes and coins to various bank branches in their area of operation.

4. Usage
The note then reaches Indians who use it for their day-to-day economic activities.

5. Return to Central Bank
When a note becomes old, soiled, or damaged, it is often returned to the bank by the public. The bank then sends these notes back to the RBI.

FINSHOTS
Subscribe to finshots.in

Data Source: rbi.org.in

HOW WILL INDIA'S DEMOGRAPHIC DIVIDEND PAN OUT?

With over 1.4 billion people, we are now the most populous country in the world, having overtaken China in 2023.

But this milestone gives us something to talk about – the demographic dividend. Because irrespective of whether we've overtaken China or not, there is one key thing about India's population – we have a super young population, with a median age of 28.4 years, and that means we have a very large population that's of working age. In fact, by 2030, 69% of the total population is expected to fall under this category. And in absolute terms, it will total 1.04 billion people.

That's the demographic dividend!

With more people in the workforce, we can have increased economic growth, and higher savings and investments. In the past, we've seen this play out in other countries. For instance, Japan in the 1960s, Korea in the 1980s and China in the 1990s – all of whom capitalized on the young population and supercharged their growth. On the other hand, countries in Latin America couldn't quite reap the benefits of their young population, and their growth rate remained anaemic.

This primarily boils down to two things – education and employment – something India will have to grapple with too.

Let's start with the education dilemma. How often have we heard people say that while the country churns out engineers, only a few of them have the skill sets that actually make them employable?

Well, according to a study by talent assessment firm Wheebox, 48% of all graduates are unemployable. Sure, this was their analysis after running a test for only around 375,000 students. So, maybe we can't simply extrapolate it entirely. But we've all heard the stories. And we know there's some semblance of truth to this.

One reason why this could be happening is that we have a bunch of private colleges in India which do the bare minimum to keep their racket going. Sample this from *The Indian Express* in 2020:

AICTE Chairman Anil Sahasrabudhe said that the root problem lies in the large number of private and deemed universities that are not under the purview of AICTE. 'The qualifying criteria were probably relaxed to increase the gross enrollment ratio, cater to increased demand, but no one followed up to check if the institutes were eventually following rules,' he said. Unlike engineering institutes whose intake is monitored by the apex body, there is no limit on private universities and deemed universities offering BTech courses.

That means we'll simply end up having a young population armed with 'worthless' degrees. And that's not going to help our growth in any way.

Also, only 5% of our workforce consists of formally skilled workers. This number is 24% in China.

Now the thing is, we can't really improve the quality of our workforce unless we hit our promise of spending more on education across the spectrum. See, one of the targets set by the government is to spend at least 6% of the GDP on education. But for a long time, it has been stuck at just under 3%.

This could potentially mean that we're squandering our demographic dividend. Maybe this feeds into our unemployment problem too.

The ILO says that the unemployment rate for those with either a bachelor's degree or higher is a staggering 29% in India. Maybe part of this is due to the unemployability of worthless degrees.

But remember, we expect this to be the segment that forms India's middle class and drives consumption in the country. We hope they'll land high-paying jobs and spend money on discretionary purchases and push the consumption economy forward. But if this segment is stuck in a rut, it's a bit of a bummer.

The 2021 Pew Survey says that the middle-income Chinese population that lives on $10–50 a day totals nearly 800 million. On the other hand, in India, this accounts for only 121 million people. So, the Indian consumption story we hear about often will be left wanting.

There's even an issue with low-skilled jobs. Numbers indicate that in the past few years, more people have gone back to jobs in agriculture, despite wages stagnating even here. To make ourselves a powerhouse, we need to create ninety-three million jobs in the manufacturing sector in the next twenty-five years. This isn't going to be easy.

Oh, and there's one more thing. There's actually a very important third piece in all this—women. Or rather, the participation of half of our population in the labour force. Between 2010 and 2020, the number of working women in India dropped from 26% to 19%, according to data compiled by the World Bank. CMIE (Centre for Monitoring Indian Economy) data confirms that post-pandemic, in 2021–2022, this metric dipped sharply to 9.2%. About 21 million women disappeared from the workforce.

The latest results of the Periodic Labour Force Survey (PLFS), released by the Labour Bureau in October 2023, showed a considerable increase in women's participation. In 2017–2018, the participation rate was 23.3%, and in 2022–2023, it was 37%.

But even then, women contribute only 18% to the GDP, despite comprising 48% of India's population.

But it's not all gloom and doom of course. Over the past couple of decades, many things have gone in our favour. We're now the fifth-largest economy in the world, overtaking our colonial masters – the United Kingdom. We took over the presidency of the G20 in 2023. We're attracting foreign manufacturers, such as Apple, to set up shop in India, which will push manufacturing. We're focusing on infrastructure building as a means to create more jobs. We've become a power in our own right.

But, in order to truly capitalize on the opportunity that this demographic dividend is offering us, we may have to do a lot more. Because before you know it, the fertility rate drops, people get older and the ratio skews in the opposite direction. We could find ourselves in the same position as Japan from the 1990s or the China of today. We need to prepare ourselves for that. And we have the next thirty years to do so.

WHY DO THE RICH KEEP GETTING RICHER?

Inequality is rife in India. Take a look at these numbers from the World Inequality Lab.

The top 10% of the Indian population holds 65% of the total national wealth. Out of this, the top 1% holds a staggering 40%.

Out of the 920 million Indian adults, the wealthiest ~10,000 own more than ₹22 billion in wealth – that's 16,763 times of what the average Indian holds. On the other hand, the bottom 50% holds a meagre ₹0.17 million – that's 0.1 times the national average.

There are 271 billionaires in India, with 94 of

them joining as recently as 2023. Their number has increased from just 1 in 1991, 9 in 2000 to 200+ in the 2020s. In fact, the numbers indicate that income inequality is worse than what it was during the British rule!

It's quite staggering really, and almost all research indicates that this disparity is likely to grow in the coming years. So, although we are growing (economically) as a country, the rising inequality negates the positive effect of this development. As a result, we are becoming increasingly unhappy, and so it's imperative to understand what's driving this phenomenon before we can counter its effect.

And one of the most comprehensive analysis on the subject comes from a French economist – Thomas Piketty. In his bestselling book *Capital in the Twenty-First Century*, Piketty outlines why the divide between the rich and the poor keeps increasing each day.

His prognosis is simple. When capital grows at a faster rate than the economy, it provides the perfect recipe for disaster. Think of capital as accumulated wealth – real estate, investments, land, bank deposits, that sort of stuff. When return from these assets vastly outweighs growth in the economy, it's safe to presume that this can only mean bad news for the working class. After all, growth in wages is directly dependent on the growth in GDP. So if 'r' (return on capital) > 'g' (growth in the economy) and the wealth of the 'rich folk' grows faster than the income of workers, it leads to an 'endless inegalitarian spiral'.

And the effect is further magnified when the difference between 'r' and 'g' increases. For instance, if the economy shrinks as a consequence of a pandemic and the return on capital doesn't fall as much (which it didn't during Covid-19), then you'll automatically see a rise in inequality. After all, income produced by capital tends to be concentrated in the hands of a small group of elites, whereas income from labour is dispersed over a much larger group. Therefore, we see inequality rising in tandem.

But how did we get here?

A simplistic analysis will tell you low tax rates, fewer regulations and low inflation will help your capital grow by leaps and bounds.

ECONOMY AND PUBLIC POLICY • 29

Think about it. If you have a fixed deposit and the government makes it easy to access that deposit, and didn't tax your savings too much, you can keep compounding wealth at a faster rate. Also, if you don't have to worry about price rise and inflation eating away the gains you made (via fixed deposit), then that's even better. Piketty uses this argument to show how the rate of return on capital changed during the twentieth century. In the first half of the twentieth century, the return on capital tumbled because of war and destruction of assets. In the second half, there was a steady growth in 'r', thanks to low inflation and countries actively pursuing policies to encourage investments. Meanwhile, growth in GDP moderated during this period. And while this analysis explains the disparity in high-income countries, the case for India is a bit complicated.

Piketty argues that the income share of the top 1% fell sharply from 1950 to the mid-1980s, and then it rose sharply, after liberalization in 1991. This would imply that ordinary citizens were treated better in the socialist era than the liberalization era. But that's a hard argument to follow. As Swaminathan Aiyar, an Indian economist notes, 'The poverty ratio did not fall at all between 1947 and 1977, while the population almost doubled. So, the absolute number of poor almost doubled. By contrast, fast growth induced by economic liberalization raised 138 million people above the poverty line between 2004 and 2011. Doubtless, inequality must have increased after economic liberalization, although not as much as Piketty estimates.'

So, technically not all inequalities are bad. If inequality rises at a time when the country is introducing policies to offer people better opportunities, then maybe Piketty's argument doesn't hold as much water. In fact, as an article in the *Atlantic* notes:

'In many countries, wealth grows more as a result of thievery and malfeasance than as a consequence of the returns on capital invested by elites (a factor that is surely at work, too). To channel Piketty, inequality will continue to rise in societies where 'c > h'. Here, 'c' stands for the degree to which corrupt politicians and public employees, along with their private-sector cronies, break laws for personal gain, and 'h' represents the degree to which honest politicians and public employees uphold fair governing practices. Corruption-fuelled inequality flourishes in societies where there are no incentives, rules, or institutions to hinder corruption.'

And maybe, that last line explains why the rich keep getting richer in this country.

SHOULD WE HAVE A FOUR-DAY WORKWEEK?

Picture this – it's Friday. Most of us are probably hunched over our desks working. And we're dreaming about the weekend.

But in the UK, Iceland and Belgium, some people are already spending time with their families. They're having elaborate lunches in parks, or even volunteering at their local charities. Their weekend has already begun.

These folks are living the four-day workweek fantasy in real life.

Now some people reading this will scoff at this idea. They'll call it insane and say that it's bad for the economy. And some others will even go as far as to say, 'Look at this absurdity. This is why there aren't great tech companies from Europe.' (Yup, this conversation happens all the time on Twitter, now X.)

But just think about it for a moment – Did you ever pause to wonder how we got to the five-day workweek in the first place?

Back in the 1800s, such a concept was quite alien. US factory workers were always hard at work. The employer dictated the terms, and the working hours could range from fourteen to sixteen hours. Maybe it would even be a seven-day week. And at some point, people had enough. They banded together and organized strikes. They even coined a slogan, 'Eight hours for work, eight hours for rest, eight hours for what we will.'

But most employers didn't budge.

A few trials took place in England and the US for a shorter workweek. But it took a decision by Henry Ford, the man behind the Ford Motor Company, to finally propel the change in 1926. He cut the workweek from forty-eight to forty hours. And some people say it wasn't really union pressure that forced his hand. Rather, he understood that a forty-hour workweek would make employees happier, and could even boost productivity.

But guess what actually gave a huge boost to the five-day workweek?

The Great Depression (1929)!

Back then, unemployment had gone through the roof. The US economy was in the doldrums. And the folks in power thought that if people worked less (for less money, too), the workload could be shared with the unemployed. It would at least lead to shared prosperity.

Pretty soon, people realized that this worked better for everyone. And in 1938, the US passed a law mandating the now ubiquitous eight hours a day and five days a week schedule.

Did it hurt economic output?

Not in the least bit. Countries showed phenomenal growth rates in the decades to come. And worker productivity soared.

Alright, so what's the deal with the four-day workweek then?

Well, it's still quite early to tell. But the

results seem promising, at least for now. For instance, Microsoft trialled this in Japan in 2019 and found a 40% boost in worker productivity.

In the UK, employers found that rising employee satisfaction and falling employee sickness actually resulted in savings of 2% of their sales each year. Maybe because they didn't have to deal with attrition and training costs for new employees.

And when the UAE implemented a four-and-a-half-day workweek for all government employees, the results were quite outstanding too. Absenteeism reduced by 55% and 70% of employees said they felt more productive and efficient at work, simply because they were happier.

Wait … this can't possibly work in the service industry though, right? In hotels and hospitals and such.

Well, let's look at the case of a nursing home in the US that was struggling with employee attrition. The nursing staff was exhausted by the long hours, and neither were they paid well. So the bosses decided to reduce the working hours from the existing forty to thirty hours a week. But the staff were paid for the full forty hours. Sure, they had to hire more staff to make up for this, which led to an increase in costs. But there was an indirect benefit – the infection rates of patients in the nursing home dropped and they felt more cared for.

You'd think that's good for business, right?

So yeah, fewer hours seem to be a win-win situation for everyone. At least in most cases.

But here's something we bet you didn't know.

The four-day workweeks aren't really a new idea. Nope! In fact, in 1956, Richard Nixon, who was then the US vice president, had floated the idea. And by the 1960s, more people were clamouring for six-hour days or shorter workweeks.

So why didn't the idea become more widespread?

For one, there's the crucial economic element.

The Economist plotted the hours worked against productivity per hour and found an inverse correlation – fewer the hours, greater the output. Seems reasonable, right? For people feel less burnt out and put in more effort. But, as John Pencavel of Stanford University points out, this is valid only if the number of hours worked initially is extremely high. Beyond a point, dropping the hours actually doesn't boost productivity, since people are more or less well-rested. So, dropping down from a manageable forty hours a week to less may not move the productivity needle by much in the long run.

But not everyone listens to economists, right? So there must be something else.

And that's the social aspect. Historian Benjamin Hunnicutt has a theory about changing culture: 'Job became a religion-like source of meaning for many people.' Also, 'The blossoming of advertising and consumerism around this same time which set people on a course of working more in order to buy more.' So that's the infinite loop we all find ourselves in even today.

Anyway, the four-day workweek might not be the panacea that workers hope for.

After all, if you have one day less to achieve the same output and targets as a five-day workweek, you might end up packing in more hours of work every day. And that could actually hurt your work-life balance in a big way. Your daily activities can be severely dented. You might start work at the crack of dawn and end after sunset, which might leave you with no time at all on a weekday. And, in the long run, you could end up feeling more burnt out.

Since most four-day workweek trials don't have enough history, we can't accurately gauge it's impact.

Also, from an organization's point of view, bosses are also worried that if people are laser-focused on efficiency every day, it could lead to less socializing at work. This would have a negative impact on knowledge sharing in the long run. And it could even hurt the organization's culture.

So yeah, it's quite a tricky situation. And it might be a while before we reach some sort of a consensus.

HOW DOES THE RBI CONTROL INFLATION?

MONETARY POLICY:

The RBI uses monetary policy to influence the amount of money circulating in the economy.

Monetary policy can be:

- **Expansionary** (To boost the supply of money during times of recession) or
- **Contractionary** (To reduce the supply of money during periods of high inflation).

And there are two ways the RBI does this:

QUANTITATIVE

Quantitative tools regulate the volume of money and credit within the system.

QUALITATIVE

Qualitative tools help RBI influence credit distribution and allocation within the economy.

QUANTITATIVE

1. BANK RATE:

The rate at which **collateral-free** loans are offered by the RBI to commercial banks.

WHY SUPPLY DECREASES?

RBI lending at a higher rate means banks would take less loans which will reduce the money supply in the economy.

if RBI lends at high rate

 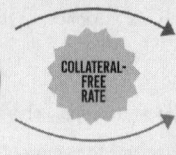 

COLLATERAL-FREE RATE

if RBI lends at low rate

WHY SUPPLY INCREASES?

RBI lending at a lower rate means banks would take more loans which will increase the money supply in the economy.

■ Money supply decreases in the economy
■ Money supply increases in the economy

QUANTITATIVE

2. OPEN MARKET OPERATIONS:

Sale/purchase of securities such as government bonds by the RBI to/from commercial banks and other organisations.

WHY SUPPLY DECREASES?

When the RBI sells securities to an entity, money is transferred from the buyer to the RBI. This reduces liquidity in the economy.

if RBI sells securities

 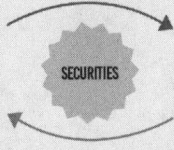

if RBI buys securities

WHY SUPPLY INCREASES?

When the RBI buys securities, money is transferred from the RBI, back to the buyer. This increases liquidity in the economy.

■ Money supply decreases in the economy

■ Money supply increases in the economy

QUANTITATIVE

3. RESERVE RATIOS:

Commercial banks are meant to maintain a certain amount (in cash/gold/government bonds) with the RBI. This amount is calculated as **percentage of a bank's liabilities** which include savings accounts and fixed deposits in

I) CASH RESERVE RATIO (CRR):

Refers to the **minimum amount of liquid cash a bank has** to maintain with the RBI.

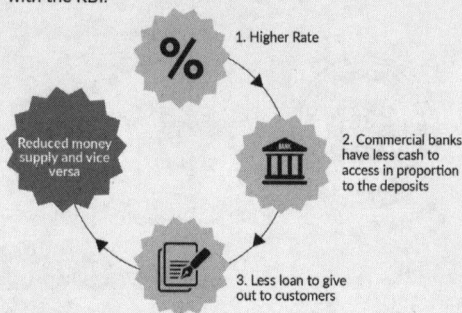

1. Higher Rate
2. Commercial banks have less cash to access in proportion to the deposits
3. Less loan to give out to customers

Reduced money supply and vice versa

II) STATUTORY LIQUIDITY RATIO (SLR):

Similar to CRR; SLR is not only maintained in cash **but also in gold and government-approved securities** etc.

ECONOMY AND PUBLIC POLICY • 43

QUANTITATIVE

4. REPO RATE:

The rate at which **collateral-backed** loans are offered by the RBI to commercial banks.

WHY SUPPLY DECREASES?

If RBI increases the repo rate, loans to banks get expensive. That means banks will take lesser loans - leading to reduced money supply.

if RBI lends at high rate
(costly loan)

COLLATERAL-BACKED RATE

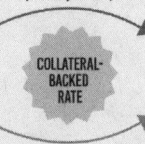

BANK

if RBI lends at low rate
(cheaper loan)

WHY SUPPLY INCREASES?

If RBI decreases the repo rate, loans to banks get cheaper. That means banks will take more loans - leading to increased money supply.

■ Money supply decreases in the economy

■ Money supply increases in the economy

QUANTITATIVE

5. REVERSE REPO RATE:

Similar to the Repo rate; however, in this case, **it is the RBI which borrows money from commercial banks.**

WHY SUPPLY DECREASES?

If RBI increases the reverse repo rate, banks are more willing to lend money to the RBI. As banks loan out more money - supply decreases in the economy.

Banks lending at high rate

Banks lending at low rate

WHY SUPPLY INCREASES?

If RBI decreases the reverse repo rate, banks are less willing to lend money to the RBI. As banks keep more of the money instead of loaning - supply increases in the economy.

 Money supply decreases in the economy

 Money supply increases in the economy

QUALITATIVE (SELECTIVE METHOD)

6. CHANGE IN LOAN-TO-VALUE REQUIREMENTS:

LTV refers to the amount of loan sanctioned in proportion to the worth of collateral given.

RBI can influence credit available to different sectors via this tool.

For instance, if the LTV is 70%, you would get a ₹70 loan for ₹100 worth of collateral.

7. REGULATION OF CONSUMER CREDIT:

This refers to loan instalments, down payment amounts, loan duration, etc.

For instance, if banks increase the minimum down payment amount required to purchase an item, it will discourage buyers from purchasing. This helps control excess spending during inflation and vice versa.

8. SELECTIVE CREDIT CONTROL:

The RBI directs banks to tweak their lending to certain industries.

For instance, an industry such as sugar could borrow at low rates and hoard the commodity. This will increase sugar prices. The RBI asks banks to control credit to this industry to keep a lid on such practices.

QUALITATIVE (SELECTIVE METHOD)

9. MORAL SUASION:

It refers to suggestions made by the RBI to commercial banks to regulate credit in the economy.

It's the **RBI's way to influence banks to act** on things like reducing their lending rates.

However, not following these recommendations will not invite penalties.

10. DIRECT ACTION:

As the name suggests, **this is an extreme step** where RBI takes matters into its own hands.

The RBI may levy sanctions and impose forceful changes to ensure that the commercial bank takes decisions in line with the monetary policy.

WHAT IS THE IMPACT OF THE THIRD GENDER ON THE ECONOMY?

In 2014, the Supreme Court ruled that transgender Indians were entitled to self-identify their gender, without having to go through invasive medical examinations. They were also entitled to a third gender status, which paved the way for their legal recognition. In 2019, the Transgender Persons (Protection of Rights) Act urged central government departments to list a third option in the gender section. So people applying for jobs now have the opportunity to mark their gender as they see fit. And in 2021,

Karnataka became the first state in India to extend reservation (1%) to the transgender community in all government services.

But despite this, they're still not well integrated into the economy.

Why, you ask?

Let's start with education. According to the 2011 census, only 46% of those who selected the 'other' gender option were literate compared to 74% of the remaining population. This could be a result of systemic discrimination, excluding transgenders from educational settings altogether or harassment, which compels them to drop out when they're young. In fact, nearly six in ten transgender persons surveyed in Kerala had dropped out of school due to 'severe harassment' and negative experiences related to their gender. And when they grow older and try to find a job, they're often unequipped to deal with the demands of high-skilled labour, because they never had a fair shot.

It's a pernicious cycle.

But on the off-chance that they do manage to get quality education, they're still denied opportunities at the workplace. A National Human Rights Commissions Survey in 2018 found that 96% of all transgender people are still denied jobs on the basis of their gender identity alone. And a few years ago, a human rights organization survey found that more than half of all transgender folks make less than ₹5,000 a month.

The problems extend to subsidies too. In 2020, as India locked down to counter the effects of the pandemic, the government promised a direct cash transfer of ₹1,500 for all transgender people, alongside ration supplies. But out of the 4.88 lakh transpeople identified during the census, only 5,711 received the bank transfer, and an even smaller subset of 1,229 transpeople received ration supplies.

This isn't because the government didn't have money. There's a more fundamental problem at play here. Most transgenders don't have a bank account. And they don't have a bank account because they don't have the right identity cards. And they don't have the right identity cards because there's inconsistency in their records.

More often than not, they have a hotchpotch of ID cards, with both their old and new names alongside their new gender. This creates confusion, which in turn may exclude them from the financial ecosystem.

What about those who've applied for a transgender certificate and an ID? According to data from National Portal for Transgender Persons, 19% of such applications are still pending, and 13.6% are marked 'not-eligible'. In the remaining lot, 32% have been in limbo for seven to twelve months. This, despite the Transgender Act making it mandatory to issue such cards within thirty days.

The point is – transpeople have to deal with harassment, systemic discrimination and social exclusion, and yet they somehow manage to make a living. It's not easy, especially when they can't even get their hands on a simple ID card.

If we can somehow solve some of their issues, they could be a valuable asset to the economy. One report indicates that sensitizing people about transgenders and others who don't conform to societal gender constructs and sexuality, could save India some $32 billion. From an economic standpoint, this can have a huge impact on the country's growth.

WERE THE 1991 ECONOMIC REFORMS GENIUS – YES OR NO?

Time and time again, there's a lot of discourse surrounding the 1991 economic reforms. So we thought it would be a good idea to trace the path to 1991 and see if the reforms deserve all that praise.

But before we get there, a reminder that a lot has been written about the matter already. And offering a simplified summary isn't very easy. So we will have to leave out many interesting details and just focus on the important bits.

Independence from British rule

It's 15 August 1947. India is finally free from the clutches of the British Empire. But as we enter this new dawn, we await a painful reckoning. The country is fragile and poor. We need to protect our people and help them move up the social ladder. And the government at the time didn't think the private industry would prioritize the needs of so many people. So they imposed restrictions – on both domestic and foreign enterprises. Most companies had to shut shop and go home, and only a select few were allowed to operate in the country. In the meantime, the government took it upon itself to power the country's economic engine. They entered manufacturing, the services industry and distribution. They were even making watches, at HMT.

Within a few years, the government intervention gave way to 'License Raj'. You needed several permits to produce even the most mundane items – soaps, TVs, you name it. And it wasn't as if these permits were doled out quickly. In fact, in some cases, it took over

400 days to obtain approvals. But that wasn't the end of it. They were also told what to produce and how much to produce. It was centralized planning at its finest.

The only problem? The consumers suffered. If you wanted a scooter, you'd have to wait for ten years! Corruption was rampant. And bribing was considered routine.

It was insane.

You can very well imagine that this didn't help the economy much. In fact, GDP growth slowed to a crawl – around 4% annually – while other developing countries, such as South Korea, were racing ahead.

India also went on a spending spree and doled out several agricultural subsidies. And after the wars with China, we were spending a lot of money on beefing up our defence. But, we weren't earning all that much because we didn't export a lot. In fact, our share of global trade fell from 2.2% in 1947 to a puny 0.45% in 1985. It was mayhem.

We kept borrowing money from external parties. Our external debt nearly doubled, from $35 billion in 1985 to $70 billion in 1990. You can imagine the heavy interest the country had to keep shelling out.

Finally, this reached a boiling point in 1990. Iraq invaded Kuwait and oil prices went through the roof.

The sins of the past had also caught up. Foreign aid wasn't forthcoming and India's dependence on NRI remittances also became an issue. Our forex reserves plummeted. And soon enough, we found out that we didn't have money to pay for imports. In fact, we had barely enough for two weeks.

India was on the brink of bankruptcy. And it was scary.

To top it all, the country was going through a phase of severe political uncertainty. The government had collapsed. Rajiv Gandhi was assassinated in May 1991. India's credit rating had been downgraded. Investors didn't want to touch India with a barge pole.

What could we do?

Well, we had a boatload of gold stashed away. And it was our last resort. The central bank used the gold as collateral, shipped them abroad and raised millions in a desperate bid to save the country.

But we were not out of the woods yet.

1991: The Eleventh Hour Transformation

When P.V. Narasimha Rao was about to assume office as India's new prime minster in July 1991, it would be trial by fire.

The situation was dire, and everyone was scrambling to figure out how we could pull ourselves out of this mess. The cabinet secretary then handed over a note to Rao. He looked at it and asked a simple question, 'Is the economic situation that bad?' The response was spine-chilling, 'No Sir, it's worse.'

That single answer apparently changed Rao – from being a staunch socialist to a champion of liberalization. Along with his Finance Minister Dr Manmohan Singh, they formulated a plan to revive India.

There were three big objectives on the agenda:

1. Devaluation of the Indian rupee: In a matter of two days, they dropped the value of the rupee by 20%. The idea was simple. If you could buy more rupees with a dollar, then somebody using the dollar abroad would find it very lucrative to import items from India. This would translate to a rise in exports at our end, and offer an avenue for us to earn foreign income (usually denominated in dollars).
2. Liberalization of trade: We cut import tariffs and substituted expensive domestic goods with cheaper foreign alternatives. Granted, this did hurt manufacturers in India. But it offered affordable options for Indian consumers. We also made it easy for foreign investors to park their money in India and Indian businesses.
3. Dismantling the Licence Raj: The private sector was given more leeway to produce stuff, and at their own will. The government refused to get involved in every aspect of production. Entrepreneurs didn't need as many permits as before, and foreign investors

were incentivized to set up businesses in India.

They basically had to take a U-turn on India's ideological stance.

And the clarion call?

Well, these were Dr Manmohan Singh's final words in the Budget speech of 1991:

'I do not minimise the difficulties that lie ahead on the long and arduous journey on which we have embarked. But as Victor Hugo once said, "No power on earth can stop an idea whose time has come." I suggest to this August House that the emergence of India as a major economic power in the world happens to be one such idea. Let the whole world hear it loud and clear. India is now wide awake. We shall prevail. We shall overcome.'

Not many realized the magnitude of these reforms. Neither did newspaper headlines scream about it.

But then, the big picture emerged. The foreign direct investment numbers in the country ballooned, from just $129 million in 1991 to $40 billion in 2005. India delivered a 'miracle' GDP growth of over 7% in just over two decades. The country's per capita income rose, from $300 in 1991 to $2,100 in 2019. And between 1990 and 2013, we pulled 170 million people out of poverty.

So, irrespective of what label we slap on the economic reforms of 1991, it is undeniably a turning point in the country's history.

The only question left is – was it all Rao and Singh?

Well, there's no doubt that the blueprint for change already existed, and many governments and ministers had dabbled with the idea prior to Rao and Singh. But until India had its back against the wall, nobody really had the gumption to execute such drastic reforms in such a short period of time. And that's precisely what Singh and Rao did when they formed an unlikely political partnership over three decades ago.

So, what do you think – were the reforms half-baked or did they boost India's quest to become an economic superpower?

WHAT IS E₹ (E-RUPEE)?

If you've been hearing about e-Rupee for a while but are still puzzled, here's a quick FAQ explainer to answer some of your questions:

1. **Is this digital money?**
   Yes.

2. **If this is digital money, how will it be any different from the digital money one transacts using UPI?**
   Now if you must transfer money over UPI, you have to make a request and forward it to your bank. The bank then decides to

deduct the balance from your account and transfer it to the beneficiary account. In the background, banks also run an elaborate clearing and settlement process to make sure everybody gets paid what they're owed and not a penny more.

So, there's a chain of intermediaries who enable this transaction.

With the digital rupee, however, you don't need any intermediaries. You could simply transfer digital money from your wallet to another wallet (belonging to an individual or a merchant), just as you would when you hand someone physical cash. The transaction is final. The settlement is final, and you may not even need an internet connection.

It's just like physical cash, only it's entirely digitized.

3. **But wait, how do I get my hands on e-Rupee?**
First, you'd need to install the CBDC (Central Bank Digital Currency) app, and use a phone number linked to a bank

account. Once you register successfully on the app, you will be assigned a digital wallet with a unique ID. You can then load the wallet by transferring money from your bank account. Now here's where things get interesting. The app will let you pick currency in any denomination. So, if you're loading ₹10,000, you could perhaps ask for the following denominations: ₹500x16 units, ₹100x10 units and ₹50x20 units.

Once you confirm, your wallet will include digital currency in these denominations.

4. **Okay, but what's the point? How will it benefit me?**

Alright, let's suppose you want to transfer a large sum of money. If you're making the transaction with a bank, it may impose restrictions on how much money you can transfer and to whom in a day. If you're sending money to a new account, you may have to wait for the bank to authorize the transaction. However, if 'digital rupee' is stored in your wallet, you should be able to transfer the money instantaneously, without a hitch – at least in principle.

The presumption right now is that it will offer users a higher degree of flexibility. It's like having a boatload of cash in your cupboard. In theory, you should be able to hand it over to anybody, if you so wish.

But since it's just like having cash in your cupboard (but in a digital form), the e-Rupee will not earn any interest if it's sitting in a digital wallet.

5. **Fair enough! But why is the government backing this?**

    Well, not just the government, even the RBI seems to think that the e-Rupee could solve some problems associated with physical cash. Think about how hard it is to print, transport, store and distribute physical money. It's a logistical nightmare and very expensive. However, if you could replace some of this cash with digital currencies, it could save the government a lot of money.

    The flip side, however, is that not everyone

is convinced that it's a more affordable alternative. If the government has to issue different denominations as digital tokens and process all the overhead, it could get more complicated and thereby more expensive. So it could swing both ways.

But perhaps the biggest benefit could include a concept called 'programmable money'. Through this, the RBI can give a specific purpose to digital money. They can say, 'This digital cash can only be used for xyz reason.'

For instance, if the government is thinking of extending fertilizer subsidies to farmers, they could load the wallet with pre-programmed money and label it as, 'e-Rupee that can only be spent on fertilizers'. They could also measure the efficacy of the programme at a centralized level, by tracking this money and seeing where people are spending it.

6. Damn, that sounds like a privacy nightmare.

Yes. But banks already track all digital transactions. So, this isn't vastly different. In fact, if anything it seems the RBI is asking banks to not report low-value e-Rupee transactions, in a bid to offer the same degree of anonymity as physical cash.

However, having said that, if we go down this route of transacting with programmable money, it could be possible for the state to impose all kinds of restrictions, which simply wouldn't be possible in the traditional banking ecosystem (or physical cash). That could be scary.

And if the e-Rupee replaces physical cash entirely, it could be very, very scary.

For now, however, we will just have to wait and see how it all pans out.

HOW DOES GOVERNMENT CONTROL INFLATION?

FISCAL POLICY:

Refers to the government's practices to make sure there's sustainable growth, price stability and increased employment levels.

The government can influence fiscal policy to be
- **Expansionary** – to boost the economy by increasing the money supply
- **Contractionary** – to keep unsustainable growth in check by reducing the money supply

Broadly speaking, there are 2 instruments of Fiscal Policy:

GOVERNMENT REVENUE (TAXATION)

GOVERNMENT EXPENDITURE

1. GOVT REVENUE (TAXATION):

Taxes (both direct and indirect) act as **a source of revenue** for the government. Taxes also have a second-order impact on the economy.

WHY SUPPLY DECREASES?

If inflation is due to high private spending — **higher tax rates reduce the purchasing power among people.** This leads to reduced expenditure and ultimately reduces the money supply.

High Tax Rates

सत्यमेव जयते
Goverment Of India

Low Tax Rates

WHY SUPPLY INCREASES?

If recession is due to low private spending — **lower tax rates increase the purchasing power among people.** This leads to increased spending and ultimately increases the money supply.

- Money supply decreases in the economy
- Money supply increases in the economy

2. GOVT EXPENDITURE:

Given the scale on which the government can spend; government expenditure has a direct impact on the economy. Especially sectors such as defense, health, education, and law and order.

WHY SUPPLY DECREASES?

If inflation is triggered due to high public spending — **reducing govt expenditure could reduce consumption of public goods & services.** This ultimately reduces the money supply.

Lower Government Spending
(Lower stimulus in the economy)

Goverment Of India

Increased Government Spending
(Increased stimulus in the economy)

WHY SUPPLY INCREASES?

- Money supply decreases in the economy
- Money supply increases in the economy

If recession is due to low public spending— **increasing govt expenditure could lead to rise in consumption of public goods & services.** This ultimately increases the money supply.

SHOULD INDIA PRINT MORE CURRENCY IF WE NEED MORE MONEY?

For the uninitiated, advocates of the Modern Monetary Theory argue that countries that have the power to issue their own currency can technically never 'run out of money'. They contest that the government can spend on food, healthcare, infrastructure and other essentials without having to worry too much about the debt burden (fiscal deficit, more specifically).

And even though the theory seems to fly in the face of well-accepted ideas, it isn't that radical either. Many countries spend more than they earn. In India, we've been running a deficit for ages now, and on many occasions the central bank (RBI) helps control the burden by printing more money.

In some cases, we even breach thresholds that are considered sacrosanct. For instance, during times of war or Covid, we have the provision to borrow beyond our means. And while traditional economists would caution us from straying too far with this experiment, modern monetary theorists argue that governments shouldn't worry too much about such debt.

Take, for instance, the US government. As of April 2024, the public debt of the United States stood at $34.61 trillion dollars. This is a gargantuan sum by any account. However, proponents of the theory will argue that the US shouldn't have to worry about the debt because they can always pay back the creditors using the dollars they can print. They're the only authority that can do this, and so technically all they have to do is print new money to pay back their debt.

And this is where things get interesting. If you've been a Finshots reader for a while, you'll say something like this: 'When you offer anything in abundance, the value of the said commodity must depreciate. Offer a person too much attention, and maybe they won't value you as much. Circulate a ton of money, and maybe the dollar will suffer the same fate. It's the law of demand and supply. If all the freshly minted money makes its way into the hands of people, the value of the dollar may tumble. You'll have to pay more to get less. While once you could buy a gallon of milk for $2, you'll now have to shell out $4. Ergo, there is a very real risk of stoking inflation.'

But modern monetary theorists argue that governments don't have to worry about this too much since they've been printing money for almost a decade now, without triggering runaway inflation. So the question then is: Why can't India pursue such a programme?

Well, because the Indian currency does not enjoy the same status as some of the other currencies.

For instance, the Federal Reserve (US Central Bank) can keep printing and pushing more dollars into the ecosystem, simply because there's always more demand for the currency. Americans use it. Foreign investors buy it. Big corporations trade with it. And considering there is almost an overwhelming consensus that the US economy is more stable than other emerging economies, the US can simply get away with it.

India doesn't enjoy the same status. So there's always a risk that an emerging economy like ours could potentially trigger inflation if we simply threw all caution to the wind. Then there's the fact that we also have to contend with a current account deficit – which usually happens when we import more than we export. See, although we have the luxury to borrow in our own currency, we can't always use it for trade. For instance, we must pay in dollars while buying oil and other stuff from foreign nations. And, if we constantly print more money in a bid to facilitate extravagant spending, then we run the risk of devaluing our currency. In that scenario, we will need more rupees to buy the same amount of dollars and importers will have to pay a steep price for the government's misadventure.

So yeah, Modern Monetary Theory might hold merit for some economies, but for the likes of India, maybe not so much.

HOW DO INTEREST RATES IMPACT OUR ECONOMY?

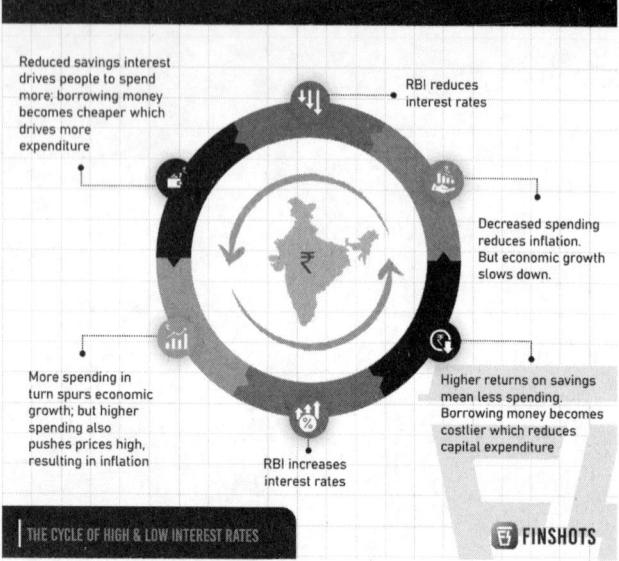

WHAT IF WE ABOLISHED THE INCOME TAX?

Some time back, a reader of Finshots left a very interesting comment on one of our articles. It went something like this: 'Why can't we just eliminate income tax altogether and compensate it with a higher GST? Shouldn't this ideally expand the tax base and improve collection overall? Think about the benefit of not having to go through the whole charade of filing your IT returns.'

The logic is very compelling, and the argument does sound foolproof. After all, if you have an opportunity to compel people to pay taxes based on their consumption patterns, that should solve most of our problems. People who earn a king's ransom are likely to splurge, and a consumption-based sales tax (like GST) will capture this information, that is, a higher spending should get them to cough up more GST. On the flip side, somebody who manages to barely make ends meet won't have to worry too much, since their consumption levels are already moderate. They will pay GST in line with what they consume. This shouldn't be too much of a burden.

But what if it is? What if the poor end up shouldering a higher tax burden?

In fact, all evidence points to this eventuality. If the income tax is abolished, an average Joe will end up paying much more than they would have otherwise, while the rich would get off much easier. That's what the data keeps telling us. This is completely antithetical to the idea of a progressive tax regime, where a higher tax rate is imposed on the rich based on their income, and offers people with 'little to no income' additional respite. With a flat consumption-based tax rate, this premise would not be feasible anymore.

But what if we switched it up a bit? What if the government compensated those living near the poverty line and offered them extra leeway. For instance, one idea that's gained significant traction in the US is the idea of implementing a fair tax regime. At its core, it is a consumption-based tax (like the GST), which is fixed at 23%. However, to make it more progressive, the fair tax act proposes to offer some people money upfront – equal to the 23% tax levied on the monthly cost of living at the poverty level. So if you are a family of four and living near the poverty line, and make $24,000, you'll be offered $5520 upfront (paid on a monthly basis). This alleviates the burden at the bottom of the pyramid and makes the whole system more equitable.

So why not just implement a similar system in India and abolish income tax altogether?

Well, you could. But doing so would mean pushing GST rates higher across the board. This translates to expensive healthcare, expensive bread, expensive rotis, expensive education (if it's not considered an investment). The government will then have to offer exemptions on some products or risk facing public wrath. However, offering exemptions would inevitably mean extracting a higher sum from elsewhere. So GST rates on other taxable products and services will rise exponentially.

Also, replacing income tax with a consumption-based tax doesn't necessarily imply that tax evasion would disappear overnight. With high GST rates, people will have every incentive to report their transactions as business transactions. And a business expense isn't taxed, for the obvious reason that the company doesn't consume the product itself. In most cases, it adds value and passes it on to the end consumer, who's responsible for shouldering the tax burden.

And as more people resort to these shenanigans, the government will have to offset the losses incurred by pushing GST rates even higher. One could also contend that marking these transactions as business expenses is no easy task for a middle-income consumer. The only people who could get away with this are probably sitting at the top of the pyramid.

So in effect, we are looking at steep GST rates on a select set of products and services, paid predominantly by the middle class. Could it work? Maybe. But is it worth the effort? That we do not know.

WHAT IS INHERITANCE TAX? IS IT A GOOD IDEA?

'If one has $100 million worth of wealth and when he dies he can only transfer probably 45% to his children, 55% is grabbed by the government. That's an interesting law. It says you, in your generation, made wealth and you are leaving now, you must leave your wealth for the public, not all of it, half of it, which to me sounds fair.'

That's Sam Pitroda's take on inheritance tax.

And unless you've been living under a rock, you probably know that this man, who's a telecommunication engineer, entrepreneur and also a former advisor to late former Prime Minister Rajiv Gandhi, had sparked a political row with this statement.

So let's look at it objectively. Is there a case for inheritance tax or is it just a bad idea overall?

Well, for starters, many institutions believe inheritance tax does have a place in the global economic system. In fact, it's something even the OECD (Organisation for Economic Co-operation and Development), an intergovernmental organization, builds a case for.

If you're wondering why, the simple answer is income inequality. Here's a rudimentary example:

Just imagine that half of the world's population is rich and the other half poor. Now, let's assume that one person from each of the categories dies. What do you think would happen?

Well, the rich would pass on their accumulated wealth to their heirs, who didn't really have to work to earn it. It's free money, and they can do whatever they wish to do with it. On the flip side, the poor who died wouldn't be able to pass on much to his kith and kin. The heirs will have to work hard to break out of the cycle of poverty.

And as of 2021, the wealthiest households (or the top 20%) in OECD countries have received close to fifty times higher inheritances and gifts as compared to the poorest households (or the bottom 20%). So, there's little wealth that can multiply amongst the poor. This means that the economic divide between rich and poor only grows wider. This can be a problem in any society.

Enter inheritance tax.

The tax can help narrow down the economic divide, because the government can add this revenue to its coffers and simply redistribute it to the poorer sections of the society, in the form of social welfare schemes. So, though it doesn't sound great for the rich, it could bridge the economic divide to an extent.

A 1993 study called The Carnegie Conjecture found that people who received large amounts of inherited wealth were more likely to exit the labour force. Even if they continued to remain in the labour force, their earnings grew slowly, because they'd rely on their inherited wealth and put in lower working hours as a result. So, an inheritance tax can potentially push heirs of the wealthy to earn their wealth by continuing to work.

Now, that may not seem too bad. But another 2018 study also found that for every Euro of revenue raised from inheritance taxes, the government obtains an additional €0.09 of labour income tax revenue (in net present value), as a result of higher labour supply.

These basic arguments are probably why a handful of countries, including the UK, France, Germany, Belgium, Japan, South Korea, Singapore and some states in the US, have some form of inheritance tax. It could be in the form of an inheritance tax that's charged directly to the heirs who inherit their deceased parents' or relatives' wealth. Or an estate tax that's slapped directly on the deceased, by getting them to part with a portion of their wealth, which then goes to the government. Or even a wealth tax that targets the rich, depending on the value of the assets they hold at the end of every year.

Now, it isn't that India hasn't experimented with this. In fact, we did have inheritance tax in the form of an estate tax, way back in the day, which was struck down in 1985, after nearly three decades.

But why?

According to the then Finance Minister V.P. Singh, it didn't actually help reduce the unequal distribution of wealth, or support states in financing development schemes for the poor. On the contrary, the government barely collected ₹20 crores as revenues from this tax in FY85, which represented a measly 0.4% of the total direct tax collection. And splashing money in the form of administrative costs to recoup that drop in the tax ocean simply didn't make sense.

So why is this even a debate again? Well, one argument is that the tax laws weren't well thought out back in the day.

It's also something the OECD points out. It believes that if governments have foolproof laws, taxing inheritances can actually give them a cost-benefit advantage (as opposed to wealth taxes), simply because inheritance tax is a one-time payment. So, there can't be too much ambiguity or even litigation that can arise from it. However, since wealth taxes are charged every year, it could turn out to be an expensive proposition for governments, since it can be hard to sort out administrative issues, like taxing jointly held assets by multiple legal heirs.

But then there's the other side of the coin. Inheritance taxes can be deeply problematic. Nobody wants to part with their wealth, especially when the primary motivation for generating such wealth could be their heirs. It could also leave less money in the hands of the heirs of the ultra rich, reducing investments they may make into businesses. And that could spiral into lower job creation and lower savings, hindering economic growth. It's also why the US government's opposition party (the Republicans) slipped in a bill (in 2024) to repeal the existing Death Tax laws.

And that's not the only argument against it. When an inheritance tax is levied, what do you think would be the first thing the rich would do?

They'd probably try to change the timing of when they transfer wealth to their children. In some cases, they'll transfer it inter vivos, or when they're alive, if such taxes are lower than the inheritance taxes their children will have to bear. Otherwise, it'll be moved to some form of a tax-exempt trust, which will make the transfer to their heirs easier.

But that isn't even the biggest drawback. Inheritance tax can actually get the rich to park money or wealth in tax havens. They might even choose to give up their citizenship and buy a passport in a country that doesn't go after their wealth. That will lead to a flight of wealth from the home country, too.

So yeah, if such gaps aren't closed, it might defeat the purpose of an inheritance tax.

Also, this isn't a new debate, and you can be sure it'll crop up again.

WHAT IS THE IMPACT OF LONG NOTICE PERIODS?

Now, you probably know what a notice period is. You let your employer know you're leaving by putting in your resignation letter, and then serve for a bit of time before leaving for good. And during this time, you help the company transition.

But why do companies even have notice periods?

Look, when you formally break the news of your intention to quit, your company might not always be ready for it. It needs to hire someone capable enough to fill the vacancy you created. And it could take them days or even months to do that.

On the other hand, if it allows you to leave immediately, it could lose a lot of money due to the temporary work suspension in your absence. So, if you decide to leave without serving your notice period, you are expected to compensate your employer.

Notice periods aren't meant to penalize anybody. In fact, their objective is to protect employees, too, as it gives them time to look for new opportunities. Unfortunately, notice periods have been painted in a bad light, and they seem to be the centre of a cold war between employers and employees.

For instance, the average notice period for the Indian IT sector is ninety days. This can seem like a very long time, especially if you have a job offer in hand. Your new employer might want you to join immediately, while you're stuck, serving a notice period that feels like an eternity.

And according to Gaurav Chattur, co-founder of Catenon, a talent consulting firm, there's logic behind this. Employers believe that they can control their employee retention rate if they hold you on the job longer. A long wait time can discourage others from recruiting you. That way you are also likely to change your mind and withdraw your resignation.

But funnily, this could backfire. An employee who's leaving might not be as committed to their responsibilities. They could even distract peers with their shiny new job offer, which could encourage others to follow suit. Now, a lot of employees quit their jobs every year. The attrition rate has drastically risen from 6% in 2020 to 18% in 2023. This includes companies asking employees to leave, too. But the end result is that long notice periods could translate into economic costs worth over $5 billion for the employer itself. Courtesy, lost productivity linked to long notice periods.

But that doesn't deter employers from playing fast and loose with notice periods. They might choose what they think suits them best. And they have the liberty to do so because there isn't really a law or regulation that governs notice periods in India.

The Industrial Disputes Act, for example, doesn't define a notice period. It also refers to a termination as retrenchment. In that case, an employer must give a workman at least a month's notice before asking them to leave. Indian states, too, have their respective state's Shops and Establishments Act. And most states stick to a one-month notice period, whether it is an employee quitting voluntarily or the other way around.

So, your employer can actually ask you to stay for a month, or even longer, before you quit. You cannot sue them because no law prevents them from holding you back for three months, six months or even a year. And if you think that lengthy notice periods are only an Indian problem, here's what you should know.

Though the US has a short notice period of about two weeks, it isn't etched in law. But there are other developed economies that have long notice periods. The UK has a regulation that mandates a notice period of at least a week before you leave. But that's just the minimum. In case an employer terminates your work contract, they have to give you a notice of anything between one and twelve weeks, depending on how long you've worked. So, if an employee has an advantage when they're fired, the employer too could use the law to their advantage.

Something similar happens in Portugal and the Netherlands as well. Notice periods can be as short as one month in both countries, but longer depending on an employee's history with the company.

That might be enough proof to say that even a uniform regulation may not help shorten notice periods. In some cases, a notice period may be warranted because different companies spend different amounts of time training their employees. And they spend a lot of money on these sessions. However, it gets deeply problematic when employers use it as a tool to prevent employees from pursuing better opportunities.

So what's the solution, you ask?

Well, you could choose to sit and talk with your prospective employer if you think that your employment contract demands an unfairly long notice period. Or, you could read through your employee agreement when you decide to take up an offer. If your company values you, they will definitely be willing to negotiate on this front.

So yeah, ultimately notice periods will likely remain a contentious contractual obligation between the employer and the employee, and it doesn't look like it will change anytime soon.

WHAT IF WOMEN WERE PAID FOR DAILY CHORES?

$10.8 trillion.

That is the estimated value of unpaid labour attributable to women around the world. We're talking about things such as household chores, childcare and caring for the elderly.

But if you ask most people about unpaid labour, their responses would probably be 'It's just housework.' Or worse, 'She's just doing her duty'.

Unfortunately, housework has long been a task that's delegated to women. So while women in India spend 297 minutes per day on household chores, men spend a mere thirty-one minutes. The disparity is stark.

Now, the objective of this chapter is twofold. One, to quantify the compensation women ought to receive for the kind of work they do. Two, to figure out how to compensate them.

Let's address the first question – how do you calculate the value of unpaid labour?

Well, most people recommend the 'Time-use survey'. Basically, you actually ask women about the kind of work they do around the house. And then, calculate how much labour value would have gone into those tasks if someone was hired to do them.

Reasonable enough, right?

But some people argue that when surveys are conducted, one may not get the right answers from most women. They might believe that certain tasks are ought to be done by them. That they have no choice. And they may not consider it as work, and might not report it. For instance, they may ignore the time spent caring for a child or tending to the cattle in the house, even though both are productive work that contributes to the economy.

And if you ask India's courts, they have their own methods. When cases around negligent driving and subsequent deaths go to court, judges have sort of determined what an appropriate compensation is. I'm talking about cases specific to when women homemakers are victims of negligent driving. The judges take into account the opportunity cost – or what a woman might have earned in the job market, given her education qualifications. They consider the minimum wages for labour, and make some adjustments for age and number of children in the family.

And they've awarded compensations that range anywhere from ₹5,000 to ₹9,000 a month.

Now, one could argue that this doesn't seem like much. Or, that there are flaws in the calculations. But at least there's some precedent for calculating such payments.

Then there's the other question that everyone dreads – who pays for it?

Well, one suggestion is that the government bears this cost.

Hold on – you could argue that it would put a

lot of pressure on government coffers. But what if you were to assume that the government is only sharing the benefits of what it has reaped? As Indira Hirway, a professor of economics, wrote in *The Hindu:*

'Unpaid work also subsidises the government by taking care of the old, the sick and the disabled. The state would have spent huge amounts in the absence of unpaid work. Unpaid work is a privately produced public good, which is critical for the sustenance of the mainstream economy.'

So, you could argue that the state has an obligation to do something about this. In fact, political parties in the states of Tamil Nadu, Kerala and West Bengal have included 'payment to homemakers' in their election manifesto, too. We don't know whether it'll ever come to fruition. But it's a start, nevertheless.

Of course, if we were being honest, this is still a stretch, because these payments would inevitably cripple our finances, and not everyone agrees that these monetary payments will work to bring parity.

Some economists think that it will keep women confined to the house even more. If people believe that women are getting paid by the government for housework, why should they bother to work outside? Why should they have a career of their own?

And while the labour force participation rate of Indian women is only 37%, it could fall further as a result.

Also, cash transfers might be a problem, because men end up managing the money and making financial decisions at the end of the day. The women do not benefit.

So what's the way out then, you ask?

Well, some suggestions involve in-kind transfers, which could have a direct impact on their lives and reduce the burden of their daily chores.

For instance, providing cooking gas cylinders to each household reduces the time that women spend collecting firewood. Or, if free childcare centres are available, it reduces the burden of childcare on mothers. Take Uruguay for instance. When the country introduced the Care

Act, it changed everything. It made it a right for children and elderly persons to get care. The government took up the responsibility to provide these services, and even ensured their quality.

Other countries, too, have experimented with such unconventional policies for unpaid labour. For instance, in Belgium, the government doled out vouchers to people who hired an agency to do their housework. It was a subsidy of sorts. Finland, Sweden and Denmark have chosen to give tax breaks in similar cases. It seems to have worked in Sweden, because people who opted for the subsidies grew in their careers. They even earned $2,000 more annually.

Maybe in societies like India, where patriarchy is so deeply entrenched, we need to get men involved in sharing the housework, by giving them mandatory training and financial incentives for sharing housework. Or maybe even formalizing things, such as a mandatory paternal leave, so that men realize that they're expected to help in child-rearing, too.

Anyway, we don't know the right answer. But we're glad that people are talking about unpaid labour and ways to deal with it. Because as Prabha Kotiswaran, a professor of law and justice at King's College London, says, 'At the current rate of change – the average gender gap between the time men and women spent on unpaid work in seventy-two countries reduced by seven minutes between 1997 and 2012 – it would take 210 years for housework to be shared equally.'

We don't want to wait for over two centuries for the miracle to happen, no?

PS: The Malayalam movie *The Great Indian Kitchen* perfectly encapsulates the expectations that all Indian families place on women to do the household work.

WHERE DID INDIA'S MISSING MONUMENTS GO?

Here's a mystery – 50 of India's 3,693 centrally protected monuments are missing!

At least that's what the Ministry of Culture told the Parliament in December 2022. Heritage sites such as the Kos Minar in Haryana, the Barakhamba Cemetery in Delhi, the Ruins of the Copper Temple in Arunachal Pradesh and the Gunner Burkill's Tomb in Uttar Pradesh are nowhere to be found.

Now, you're probably wondering, 'These are gigantic monuments! Not a piece of candy that you're looking for in the fridge. How the heck could they go missing?'

Well, let's just say we didn't spend enough time looking after the monuments in the first place. We were careless.

And part of the blame lies in rapid urbanization. See, India's population has ballooned over four times since Independence – from 340 million to 1.4 billion. Another problem is land, which is limited, and we have to make do with what we have. That meant building living spaces and constructing dams and reservoirs wherever we found the space. And oftentimes, we simply didn't pay heed to these historical monuments. We razed them to the ground or submerged them. And the hidden pages of history got erased forever.

For instance, once upon a time, Delhi's Barakhamba cemetery was a tomb, named after the twelve pillars supporting its roof. But now it's on the list of untraceable monuments.

A few years ago, journalists from the *Mumbai Mirror* tried to do some digging. They found the Barakhamba Road. But there was no cemetery in the vicinity. Instead, there was a cemetery of sorts in the Nizamuddin area of Delhi. And to their surprise, it had morphed into the Ghalib Park, with a dilapidated structure in the middle and a couple of graves. That's it.

So, where did the Barakhamba cemetery disappear?

Well, one theory comes from an ASI (Archaeological Survey of India) archaeologist. In 1914, he wrote that the building was used by a government official who was a part of the team planning the city of New Delhi. In his own words, 'It is being used as an office of an executive engineer of the third project division, and has been repaired, paved and whitewashed.' Over time, people squatted in the building, and soon it gave way to a park. All that remains of the cemetery now is the road named after it.

And this is just one instance, mind you. Imagine this happening to monuments across the country.

But this begs the question – What is the economic impact of these missing monuments?

Look, monuments attract tourism. And as per the World Tourism Organization, culture and heritage motivate 40% of international tourism.

Although there isn't an exact figure that we can peg on India's cultural tourism, you can't deny that our rich culture and heritage have a huge hand in attracting tourists.

So protecting these historic sites and ruins can pep up India's tourism revenue. For instance, according to a disclosure by the Ministry of Culture, India earned about ₹93 crores in FY16, ₹225 crores in FY17 and ₹269 crores in FY18 from entry fees.

But here's the catch – we're also burning cash to look after our heritage sites. Because, during those same years, the ASI spent approximately 150%, 30% and 50% over and above its income to conserve, preserve and maintain the monuments.

On the face of it, it may not seem to be an economically viable proposition. But remember, only 116 of these monuments were ticketed, which means that entry to 97% of the centrally protected monuments was free.

So maybe just increasing the number of ticketed sites could generate revenues, which could help maintain the free sites too. Or even coming up with innovative ideas, similar to the one implemented at the iconic Taj Mahal. In December 2018, a separate entry fee of ₹200 was introduced for tourists who wished to see the main mausoleum housing the graves of the Mughal royals. It netted the ASI an additional ₹17 crores.

And such fees from iconic monuments might be imperative, as they help keep entry to other monuments free. Apparently, people's taste in tourism is changing. Niche heritage sites are having their moment in the sun. For instance, the monuments in Mamallapuram, a town close to Chennai, received about 1,06,000 more foreign tourists than the iconic Taj Mahal in FY22.

So, maybe if we preserve and promote our lesser-known heritage sites, we could see a boom in cultural tourism. Those offering public transport at these sites, such as autorickshaws and cabs, could earn better. Hospitality and handicraft revenues could go up too. It's a win-win situation for everyone. We may not even have to weigh up the economic paradox of saving a monument versus forgetting its existence.

But for all this to truly work, the government needs to pay more attention to the ASI – it needs more funds. In 2024, it got a measly ₹1102 crores for maintaining monuments, and a puny ₹3 crores in FY23 for monuments that weren't under the central protection list. You can bet this money isn't enough for upkeep.

The result? Only 7% of the centrally protected monuments have security personnel. And that's a shame, because it leads to vandalism, destruction and eventual loss of heritage sites.

The ASI also doesn't have enough power to tackle illegal encroachment of heritage sites. Maybe tweaking the law can help make them a potent monument protection force too.

Because as the Article 49 of the Constitution of India states: 'It shall be the obligation of the State to protect every monument or place or object of artistic or historic interest [declared by or under law made by Parliament to be of national importance] from spoliation, disfigurement, destruction, removal, disposal or export, as the case may be.'

So yeah, hopefully, we'll step up our game to protect these heritage sites and monuments. It's also in our economic interest to do so.

WHY DOES INDIA HAVE A PENSION PROBLEM?

There are essentially three sources of pension.

The first: You.

Every month you contribute diligently to a corpus, which of course is cut from your salary and deposited into a retirement fund. It's a 'defined contribution' plan, and you're solely responsible for building your security net.

The second: Your employer.

In some cases, your employer could help you out too, by contributing to your retirement pot every month. Sure, it takes a bite out of their revenues, but that's the cost they have to pay for engaging the services of their employees. Also, it's usually the law that forces their hand.

Finally: Current and future generations of taxpayers.

Now, this is the interesting bit. Back in the day, all retired government employees used to get a lifelong pension from the government. The pension would even be frequently adjusted for inflation. And the best part – unlike 'you', they didn't even have to contribute towards it during their tenure. It was a 'defined benefit' pension, where only the employer (the government) contributed.

But all this money had to come from somewhere, right?

When people say that it came from the government, what they actually mean is that it came from taxpayers. We were all bearing the cost of extending pensions to government workers.

But things changed in 1998, as the government realized that it simply couldn't keep asking the rest of India to pay for pensions.

For starters, some estimates say that only 1.6% of Indians are employed in the government sector, while nearly 80% of India's workforce is in the unorganized sector. The latter don't have any social security safety net of their own. Yet, their taxes too contribute to the pensions of government employees. It's not a good look.

The other 'problem' was that Indians were beginning to live longer lives. While the average life expectancy was just thirty-five years in 1950, it jumped to sixty-two years by 2000. This is only going to increase further. In fact, the UN thinks that it'll be closer to eighty-two years by the year 2100. This also means that the government would have to pay out pension for a longer period. And the increased liability could complicate things further.

So, in 1998, the government set up a committee to find a solution. It was called the OASIS Project– an acronym for Old Age Social and Income Security.

OASIS knew the answer was pretty simple – the government would have to kill the decades-old defined benefit plan. Employees would then have no choice but to contribute towards their retirement. Adapt to the times. As the report observed, that really was the only way to 'eliminate the free-rider problem of collectivist programmes.'

And though it took a while for the government to act on it, the National Pension System or the NPS finally emerged in 2004.

The scheme would work almost like the Employee Provident Fund (EPF) that we're familiar with. The employees would put in a share of their salary, and the government would put in a bit too. Upon retirement, a part of this corpus can be withdrawn at one go. The rest of it goes towards buying an annuity, which then pays out a monthly pension.

So, the NPS formulated a hybrid model of pension, which would protect a chunk of taxpayer's money from being used for pensions. Sounds perfect, no?

Well ... only on paper.

You see, some employees who were enrolled in the NPS many years ago are now retiring, and they think the pension payouts are quite horrendous. In fact, in 2021, an employee union gave an example of a defence employee who retired with a basic pay of ₹30,500. They said that under the old system, he would've been entitled to a monthly pension of ₹15,250, but under the NPS, his pension amount was a meagre ₹2,400.

The unions called it 'an atrocity', and demanded that states revert to the Old Pension Scheme (OPS), which would give them a defined benefit. Some states (such as Rajasthan) obliged.

But there's a problem. A pretty big one.

States are already burdened by pensions. When the *Economic Times* crunched the numbers, they found that pension already eats up over 25% of the state tax revenues. So, if every state decides to go back to the defined benefit pension, it would be mayhem, and by 2047, 40.5% of the tax revenues would be spent on pensions alone.

Now, you don't need an economist to tell you that going back to the OPS sounds like a massive commitment.

If states spend almost everything they earn on pensions, they would have no money left for building crucial infrastructure – roads, hospitals, educational institutes. They will then have no option but to keep borrowing money from the Centre. It's a debt trap.

But wait ... states aren't stupid. They've seen the reports advising them against making the shift to OPS. So why are they still considering it?

Well, it's complicated.

Under the OPS, the state governments don't really have to set aside money into a fund every month. They can postpone it till the time it is actually due. To meet the pension requirements, they could perhaps borrow money ten years from now.

In the NPS, however, as part of their contribution, states have to set aside funds immediately. The money flows out of the account today, and the expense cannot be delayed.

So, if they make the switch and go back to the OPS, their finances immediately look better. They might even save 7–10% of their pension expenditure. Their financial statements look better, and they can claim to be fiscally responsible.

But you and I know that they're simply

delaying the inevitable. It's a tradeoff – short-term gain for serious long-term pain. And no one put it better than Montek Singh Ahluwalia, an economist and former deputy chairman of the erstwhile Planning Commission: 'The big advantage for those who push this move is that the bankruptcy would come 10 years later.' It becomes someone else's headache.

And finally, you could also argue that it's all about politics. But will this come back to bite future generations?

Well, we will let you decide that.

HOW IS THE UNION BUDGET OF INDIA PREPARED?

Every February, the country is abuzz with the talks of the Union Budget. Okay, that may not be entirely true. But within select circles, people anxiously wait to see what the finance minister has in store for the Budget. So, we thought we would have a look at how India's annual financial report is actually prepared, and in the process help you understand the enormous significance of this little document.

But before we do that, let's take a quick look at the basics of budgeting, taking the example of how you prepare your household budget. First, you tally all your sources of income – salary, money that a friend has promised to repay you, earnings from a YouTube video you managed to monetize, etc. Anything you can count on. Then you map out your expenses – rent, EMI, your cook's salary, etc. Ideally, you wouldn't want to spend beyond your means. But, if you have some heavy-duty expenses lined up, you will have to breach the limit and resort to outside borrowing.

You might also choose to discuss with your financial advisor how best to invest your money and allocate your spending. You might even have a chat with your cook to cut down on grocery expenses. In summary, you will use all your sources of income to plan both routine and singular expenses for the whole month, in consultation with stakeholders who might influence your spending patterns. This is essentially how the government budget is planned as well, just on a much, much larger scale.

The Union Budget is essentially the statement of the government's income and expenditure for a financial year. It details how much money the government expects to raise in the upcoming financial year, and how it's planning to allocate it among different states, departments and sectors. Of course, they have to take a lot of things into account – how much money the state governments need, what are the top priority sectors, how tax revenue could be maximized, how the general standard of living can be improved, etc.

Since the Budget affects billions of people, the central government can't really do it alone. The ministry of finance consults with the government's think tank NITI Aayog, and different spending ministries like defence, education, home affairs, etc., in order to arrive at the Budget document.

The process starts five to six months before the Budget is presented. The finance ministry sends spending guidelines to all the stakeholders – ministries, states, union territories, autonomous bodies, departments, and the defence forces. They evaluate their respective needs and write back to the government elaborating their demands.

Then the finance ministry holds meetings with key stakeholders, such as farmers, economists, civil society groups and businessmen, to understand their views on how best to allocate resources to their specific sectors.

The revenue-earning ministries then provide three kinds of figures for both income and expenditure, detailing how much they actually spent during the previous Budget year, revised figures according to the actual rate of spending in the ongoing year and how much they expect to spend during the upcoming year. The budget department consolidates these figures and prepares the final document.

And then they eat some halwa and chill.

No, we're not kidding. The finance minister and other officials do participate in a traditional 'halwa ceremony', which marks the beginning of the actual printing of the document. After this, whoever is directly associated with the Budget is required to stay in the ministry for nine to ten days, completely cut off from the outside world, until the Budget is presented. On the day of the budget presentation, the finance minister takes the permission of the president to present the Budget to the Parliament, and the Parliament then discusses the Budget.

HOW DOES THE RBI MAKE MONEY?

The RBI is a not-for-profit organization.* Yet, it made a profit of nearly ₹2.5 lakh crores in FY24!

How on earth did it achieve this, you ask?

Through the simple process of seigniorage.

---

* Not technically, but let's just assume that it's a not-for-profit. Because the RBI's goal isn't profits. Rather, it needs to manage inflation and keep it under control, so that we don't have to pay through our noses to purchase the basics. It also has to help push growth in the economy. And, it also needs to get people to believe in the value of the rupee. Put simply, the goal is to ensure monetary stability. So, even though RBI can print as much money as possible, it can't keep doing so, because that would mess with the RBI's ultimate goal – price stability.

Now this is just a fancy term for the profits that the bank makes by printing currency. Think about it this way. If the RBI prints a ₹100 note and gives it to a bank for circulation, the bank doesn't get it for free. It has to 'buy' the note, and transfer the full face value of ₹100 to the RBI's coffers.

But here's the thing. The RBI basically whipped this note out of thin air. The only cost it incurred was to print the note, probably around ₹2. Put another way, the RBI spent ₹2 and created ₹100 in face value, and the profit for the central bank is derived from putting that ₹100 to good use. That profit is called seigniorage.

So what does it do with these profits?

Well, it puts the money to good use and tries to make even more money for itself. For instance, it can lend this money to banks for their daily needs. This fetches interest for the RBI. Then there's the government, which also needs money for its activities. And when the government issues bonds to borrow money from people, the RBI steps in here, too. It buys these bonds and pockets a nice sum of interest from the government.

The RBI can also buy foreign assets, such as US government bonds. It earns interest and has the benefit of giving the RBI some exposure to the dollar. Or it can even buy and hold dollars on its own. When the value of the dollar rises, the RBI can act proactively, sell them, and pocket the gains. In fact, just by buying low and selling high, the RBI made over ₹1 lakh crores in forex trades in 2023.

Basically, the RBI prints or creates a bit of money and then uses that to make a whole lot more.

The end result of all this is that the RBI earned a grand total of ₹2.75 lakh crore in FY24.

It gets to pocket most of this because it doesn't have too many expenses either. There is the cost of printing notes. Then, it delegates some form of government-related work to other banks, and pays them a fee for their services. And finally, it needs to pay everyone on its payroll. Put together, this comes up to just about ₹20,000 crores.

And since the RBI isn't really a 'for-profit' entity, it doesn't pay any income tax.

Ergo, the massive profits of ₹2.5 lakh crores!

Now, the RBI is a prudent money manager. So when it makes a windfall, the first thing it does is save a chunk of it for a rainy day. It pushes the money into its contingency fund. Something it can dip into if there's an unprecedented event that rocks the economy—say if some of its investments fail or a pandemic hits again, and we need to protect the banking system.

In 2024, it decided to move ₹0.42 lakh crores into this fund as a safety net.

Now if you jot these numbers down on a spreadsheet, you'll see that there's still some money left over in its coffers. In fact, the net income for the RBI was approximately ₹2.1 crores in FY24.

But it doesn't really keep this for itself, either. Instead, it transfers it to the government as dividend.

See, typically, the government spends more than it earns. It needs to build infrastructure, dole out subsidies for social welfare schemes and beef up the military... there are a whole lot of expenses. So, we end up borrowing money from the World Bank and other global financial institutes and paying interest on it. And thus, any bonus money really helps. Since the RBI is technically owned by the government, it gets its share of profits, too.

So yeah, because the RBI had quite a bonanza in 2024, not only was it able to build its contingency fund, it could even transfer ₹2.1 lakh crores to the government as dividend.

And now you know how the RBI makes and spends its money.

WHAT IS THE VALUE OF A TREE?

The economic value of a tree shouldn't be limited to the value of timber. Instead, it must encompass its lifetime contribution. Trees prevent the contamination of soil. They improve the quality of water underground. They provide natural shade. They extract carbon dioxide and offer oxygen.

A few trees in a neighbourhood can make a whole lot of difference. To begin with, it will make the place much cooler, bringing down your AC bill. Trees can also alleviate flooding risks. Old trees have heritage value. They have been around for a long time. They've seen the Great

Depression. They've seen the tricolour unfurl for the first time. They've seen bloodshed. They've seen peace. Some of them are irreplaceable. And yet, governments are often forced to uproot these national treasures in the name of development. Sometimes it's understandable. But most times, it's simply egregious.

The government has frequently relied on a rather simplistic arrangement – cut one tree and plant a few odd saplings somewhere else. That should do, right? While the logic can be appealing, this isn't exactly a like-for-like replacement.

Different trees support different kinds of ecology. There's no point replacing a sal tree with a teak. And there's certainly no point in planting a sapling and forgetting about it. Because, often times, they don't get the attention they deserve. So, there is an obvious need to look at our strategy again. And when a few years ago, the West Bengal government decided to cut 356 trees to construct five railway overbridges (RoBs), the matter was brought to the Supreme Court.

The Court had a tough task at hand. Obviously, the overbridge was deemed necessary. But then, cutting down so many trees also seemed excessive. So they put together a committee of five experts to figure out the economic value of a tree.

Here's what it recommended – the value of a tree should tally up to its age multiplied by ₹74,500. Also, according to a report in the *Times of India*, 'The true value of a tree, with 100 years of its lifespan remaining, would be ₹72 lakh... The committee said 50 trees had already been cut, but the 306 remaining trees, many of which are of heritage value, would be valued at ₹220 crores.'

You might think this valuation is bonkers. In fact, as soon as the committee's report was made available, the Court did remark that the method of valuation would bankrupt most governments. But even if the Court were to discount the value by 50%, it would still add up to a substantial amount of money, which could act as a massive disincentive for the government. Because, if they were forced to spend a ludicrous amount of money to uproot trees, they would simply seek other alternatives.

Thinking about felling 500 trees to widen a road? Maybe you will find ways to redirect traffic somewhere else. Thinking about uprooting a 100-year-old tree? Maybe you will translocate it. And even if you don't fully compensate for the trees, maybe you could invest more in planting saplings, taking care of them, nurturing them, making sure they are a like-for-like replacement.

As a species, we are in a very precarious spot. If we continue to disregard the role trees play in sustaining humanity, there's no doubt it won't really end well for us.

What do you think about the valuation? Should we now start extending this treatment to other natural resources, too?

Well, that's something to think about!

CAPITAL MARKETS

WHAT IS MODERN PORTFOLIO THEORY?

Imagine it's the 1950s. Someone comes up to you and asks, 'How would you build a portfolio of stocks?'

You may say something like this, 'I'll look at the stocks with the most potential and buy them.'

But how do you determine potential?

Well, one way to do that is to try and forecast which stocks would generate consistently high cashflows (dividends) in the future. So, you'd calculate what the total future income would be worth in today's value, just to see if there's any merit in buying the stock right now. There's a bit of math involved.

But then, Harry Markowitz comes along.

He was studying economics at the University of Chicago and needed a topic for his PhD. A random conversation with a broker got him interested in the stock markets. So, he picked up books and started scouring them for ideas. And when he read about this approach in *The Theory of Investment Value*, Markowitz felt something was amiss.

He felt that if people only cared about the returns from stocks, they'd simply buy the one stock that had the most potential. That's what any 'rational' investor would do anyway.

But he realized that's not what people did. Investors actually diversified and bought a whole bunch of stocks. They all believed in the adage, 'Don't put all your eggs in one basket.' They were trying to reduce their risk. People were risk-averse.

Also, there was one fatal flaw in how most people constructed portfolios.

For instance, you could buy ten stocks just by

looking at the highest expected dividends. And you'd think you had a diversified portfolio. You have ten stocks after all. But what if all these high-dividend stocks were from the same sector – say banking? If something spoilt the party for the banking industry, your entire portfolio would suffer in tandem. So, there's really not much diversification here.

Instead, you needed a portfolio that was truly diversified. Or as Investopedia pithily put it, 'Consider a portfolio that holds two risky stocks: one that pays off when it rains and another that pays off when it doesn't rain. A portfolio that contains both assets will always pay off, regardless of whether it rains or shines.'

That's a unique portfolio.

It would also be less risky than a portfolio created by simply adding up the risks of individual stocks (choosing some low-risk, low-reward stocks and some high-risk, high-reward stocks to diversify) in the same sector (like banking).

While that makes intuitive sense, the weird part is that there wasn't a mathematical model to create something like this back then. So, Markowitz decided to change that. He looked at how the historic prices of a group of stocks behaved in relation to each other. Did they behave in the same manner? Or did they behave like polar opposites?

He then attempted to plot the relationship between risk and reward on a chart. His goal was to create an 'efficient portfolio', one that would help investors maximize their returns, with the least amount of risk they were willing to stomach.

And just to be clear, when Markowitz spoke about risk, he meant the ups and downs in the stock price. Or what's known as volatility.

It was the first time someone had actually quantified risk and reward in a portfolio this way. And it didn't go down too well with the professors who reviewed his dissertation. They said that the theory was 'not economics, not mathematics, not business administration, and not literature'. Apparently, they felt Markowitz seemed to care more about the algorithms that could help build the portfolio, but didn't focus on the economic theory that underpinned it.

But it was still quite a brilliant dissertation. And Markowitz was awarded the PhD.

Now sure, his dissertation became quite popular. But it was primarily restricted to the academic circles. It was when he finally made it into a book (in 1959) that the theory really gained prominence. Suddenly, wealth managers began to employ the modern portfolio theory or MPT to create portfolios for their clients – focusing on maximizing return and minimizing risk.

Three decades later, in 1990, Markowitz won the Nobel Prize in Economics.

So, is the theory still valid today?

Well, there have been criticisms of MPT. Some say that while it might theoretically make sense, the changes in the relationship between stocks keep changing. And even a small change in this relationship can call for a complete revamp of stocks in the portfolio. That doesn't bode well for long-term investors. Others say that the way risk is calculated isn't quite right and needs to be updated. Author and trader

Nassim Nicholas Taleb blamed people like Markowitz for devising simplistic equations, which fooled common investors into believing that stocks were less risky than in reality.

But despite all this, people still use versions of MPT even today, and you'll find many online investment portals that proudly proclaim that they use modern portfolio theory in their models.

In 2023, Goldman Sachs came out in defence of the iconic 60:40 portfolio that emerged out of the MPT. For the uninitiated, think of it like this—if you had ₹100 and wanted a portfolio that was adequately diversified and favourable from a risk-reward perspective, you'd put ₹60 in stocks and ₹40 in bonds. Simple.

So yeah, Harry Markowitz may have bid us farewell, but it certainly looks like his MPT legacy will live on.

WHAT IS THE BUFFETT INDICATOR? IS IT FOOLPROOF?

India's stock market capitalization hit the $5 trillion milestone (roughly ₹416 lakh crores) in May 2024. We're talking about the market value of all the companies that have their stocks listed on the BSE, formerly, Bombay Stock Exchange.

That's quite an achievement because just around six months ago, it was at the $4 trillion mark.

But this milestone seems to be worrying analysts, who believe that this could be a sign of overvalued or expensive markets. How do they know that?

Well, they looked at some important metrics.

Take, for instance, the forward P/E (price-to-earnings ratio), or the ratio you get when you combine the current share prices of all the listed companies and divide them by the sum of their estimated earnings per share (EPS) over the next twelve months.

Now, if you're unfamiliar with EPS, think of it as the profit that a listed company makes for every share that its shareholders own. But with forward P/E, you don't go by the company's EPS based on its actual profits. You go by forecasts of the future profits instead.

This metric moves in one direction – upwards. For instance, the number of companies whose stock prices are trading at over fifty times their forward P/E multiples has increased ten-fold over the past decade. It simply means that these stocks are fifty times more expensive than the estimated earnings they'll generate over the next year. That could be a sign of an overvalued market.

Then you have something called the Buffett Indicator, the protagonist of our story. You've probably guessed by the name that it's an indicator coined by Warren Buffett, Berkshire Hathaway's CEO and someone you often think of when you discuss investing. Buffett proposed this indicator way back in 2001, and even called it 'probably the best single measure of where valuations stand at any given moment'.

So what's it about, you ask?

Well, it's pretty simple. The Buffett Indicator is the market capitalization seen as a percentage of the country's GDP or the value of all goods and services the country produces.

To put things into perspective, let's assume that the market value of all listed stocks is ₹100, and that the value of all goods and services a country produces is also ₹100. Then, the Buffett Indicator will be 100% or 1 (₹100 divided by ₹100). This means that the market capitalization and GDP are the same and that stocks are fairly valued. On the flip side, if stock prices rise faster than the GDP, it could potentially be foreshadowing a stock market bubble. And stock prices nosediving below the GDP could mean that the markets are cheap, signalling a buying opportunity.

And guess what the Buffett Indicator says about India's stock market right now?

It's at 154%[*] – the highest we've seen since May 2007.

Now, before you panic and think of withdrawing all your stock market investments, here's something you must know.

The Buffett Indicator may be a metric you could look at when you make your investment decisions. But is it really reliable, or foolproof for that matter?

Research by YCharts, an investment research firm, sort of tried to look for an answer. It dug up data for the US stock markets and crunched the numbers to see how accurately the Buffett Indicator predicted stock market crashes since 1971.

And here's what they found out. If you looked at major market declines in the US since 1971, this indicator gave warning signals for 50% of them. But if you went further and looked at the data since 2000, the Buffett Indicator

---

[*] As of 21st May 2024.

successfully predicted about 57% of the major market declines.

While YCharts concluded that the Indicator provided well-timed warnings of market declines, here's the catch.

YCharts made some tweaks to the data and came up with a threshold that was more suitable for the markets of the twenty-first century. So, instead of saying that markets were overvalued when the Buffett Indicator touched 100% or more, they adjusted it to about 132%.

Even if you went by that and exited your investments from the S&P 500 (an index that tracks 500 leading publicly traded companies in the US) on 30 September 2016, you'd have avoided four major market declines of 10% or more. But, you would have still missed out on about 10% of the annualized returns until June 2022. In fact, it wouldn't even give you a heads-up on the decline that came about during the global financial crisis (2007–2008)!

So, why doesn't the Buffett Indicator get it right every time?

For starters, the metric itself may be a little

flawed. Just think about it. The GDP of a country is something that you look at over a period. It measures past economic activity for either one quarter of a year or the entire year. But that's not how market capitalization works. Stock market prices move on the basis of expectations of future performance. This simply means that if a company has the potential to give you better earnings, because it has bagged a big project or a contract, its stock will move up. The opposite happens if something dents the company's ability to do well in the future. So, with the Buffett indicator, you're not really measuring two parameters that fall under the same time frame. And if you give this further thought, you'll see that forward P/E does this job pretty well.

But you could argue that profits derived from the stock markets are a factor of the GDP, simply because GDP depends on the production of goods and services, which in turn depend on land, labour, capital and entrepreneurship. Land earns rent, labour earns wages and capital and entrepreneurship earn interest and profits. When you put rent, wages and profits together, you get GDP. And stock market capitalization does depend on at least one of these components – profits.

So, it might not be like comparing apples and oranges.

But here's the thing. The Buffett Indicator doesn't consider the effect of global operations on stock markets. Let's explain. Imagine that you kickstart a company in India and list it on the stock market. In a few years, you open several global branches too. That drives up the value of your stock in the country.

Does it affect India's GDP, though?

No.

Simply because GDP measures only the value of goods and services produced within its borders. So, this could again derail the objective of the Indicator.

And it doesn't stop there. The Buffett Indicator was coined with the US markets in mind, and assumes a strong relationship between stock market performance and economic growth. But that may not make much sense in the context of the Indian economy.

If you're wondering why, just think about the percentage of households that invest in stock markets in both countries. In the US, over 58% of households own stocks, while that figure is just about 17% in India. One market is mature. The other is getting there. And market behavior in these two scenarios can vary considerably.

So yeah, no indicator can reliably tell you whether the stock market is collectively overpriced or not. If it could, then nobody would lose money in the markets, would they?

WHAT'S THE DARK UNDERBELLY OF THE STOCK MARKET?

When we decided to work on our startup, we felt there was an urgent need for reform in the Indian stock market. We firmly believed that institutions reporting on financial markets were excluding the novice retail investor base by talking about stocks, using financial lingo that was simply too hard to understand. We thought we could fix this by writing stories that more people could relate to. This was at a time when Finshots wasn't even born. It was an idea that existed only on paper. But we knew what we wanted to do – we wanted to make stocks and financial news cool.

Unfortunately, we did not have an audience to talk to, and were out in the streets desperately looking for our big break. And then, after two weeks of waiting, we received a call from a stockbroker in Ahmedabad who seemed very keen to know what we were doing to simplify finance and business for the masses. We agreed to meet at his office and entered the building thinking we could work out a business proposal, hoping that the research division in the brokerage house would find value in our stories. The gentleman who greeted us was a big, burly man with a pot belly, and spoke with the authority of a market veteran. He quietly sized us up and asked, 'Who is going to read your stuff?'

We sat there staring at each other because we didn't really have an answer, until he spoke again.

'You should start writing about SME IPO, guys. You will get a lot of traction. We will promote your stuff. Don't worry.'

He wasn't interested in our stories or the kind of content we were creating. He simply wanted us to look at the SME (small and medium enterprise) IPO (initial public offering) market in India. A few years earlier, the Government of India had initiated a proposal to help SMEs list on the exchanges (BSE and NSE), in the hopes of making 'retail investor money' accessible to fledgling businesses.

Unlike big businesses who have access to cheap loans and instant capital, SMEs often struggle to lift their businesses out of obscurity. So when the government green-lighted the initiative, there was considerable euphoria in the market. With the backing of the government, the exchanges got to work and an SME trading platform was put together on the exchanges. The move was lauded by everyone in the financial ecosystem. Investors were happy that they could now own a piece of the burgeoning SME market, while the promoters of these small enterprises rejoiced in the knowledge that money would be less of a problem.

C.S. Mohapatra, Department of Economic Affairs, Ministry of Finance said, 'This is a big contribution to the country where SMEs play a crucial role but face difficulties in raising capital for their potential businesses. This is an effective way to improve financial inclusion.'

Dr Mohapatra was right. This was a terrific initiative to help the struggling SME industry. The hope was that once capital was made available, these small companies could scale up and add more value to the Indian economy. So, it made a lot of sense for the government to encourage such a move. But by the time we started reporting on SME stocks, the segment had devolved into an ugly business of moneymaking that lacked any significant oversight or accountability.

All That Glitters Is Not Gold

With the vote of confidence from our friendly neighbourhood stockbroker, we got to work. Our first story was on a small jewellery company involved in the business of wholesale gold. On the face of it, the company looked like it was running a tight ship. With revenues of around a few million dollars and a customer base spanning across a few hundred stores, we had no reason to believe the company was hiding anything. But once we started digging deeper, the real story started to unravel rather quickly. The company had only about ten employees. And a few months before the IPO, the CFO of the company had been working as a cashier in another jewellery company. One of the company's full-time directors, responsible for administration, was still in graduate school and was only twenty years old. Also, a significant portion of the business came from selling gold to another company, which was owned and managed by the promoters themselves. They did all this by outsourcing their entire business operation.

'I can't divulge all this information. Who are you guys?', asked the twenty-year-old director.

We tried calling the promoters, but ended up talking to the twenty-year-old director. He was confident, to begin with, but when we started pressing him about the financials, he quickly became defensive and kept insisting that he could not offer us an explanation – because that information was 'proprietary' and he couldn't divulge such matters because of legal reasons. We did not press him further.

We wrote a scathing report on the company, castigating the promoters and their business model, criticizing them for wanting to raise over a million dollars – only to then watch the retail public buy their stock and subscribe to the IPO like there was no tomorrow. The public wanted more of this company and it didn't make any sense to us. 'Who in their right mind is buying this?' scoffed Bhanu, one of our co-founders. We kept writing story after story, report after report, pointing out loopholes in these businesses and the sorry state of the company financials, only to watch the share issue get subscribed time and time again.

The Invisible Hand of the Stock Operator

It was only much later that we found out how subscriptions actually ran. Usually, it's not your average retail investor who buys shares during the primary offering (IPO). Instead, companies hire stock operators, who subscribe to the issue, bump up the price artificially post the listing and then offload them to the general public once the price becomes attractive enough for gullible investors to jump in. There is always a retail investor looking to make a quick buck from 'stocks on the rise', and once the dust settles they are often left with a dud stock, which is pretty much worthless. We spoke to one such operator, who told us in a very nonchalant manner that this was all part and parcel of the SME market, and that if it weren't for people like him, most issues would go unsubscribed.

'I don't go to promoters. They come to me. It's these guys who ask me to subscribe to the issue for a discount. If I get a 6 crore issue for 5 crores, I will buy the whole thing and operate the price,' said the 'friendly operator'.

So, the designated operator decides to bid for all the shares through his network of professionals, and then when the actual transaction is complete, the promoter returns some money to the operator as kickbacks for his service. There are good incentives for the promoter to go through with such an arrangement. If the issue isn't subscribed fully, the exchange will drop the listing and return the money raised. In that case, the promoter will end up losing a considerable sum of money (money spent on trying to list his company in the first place). So, if an operator bears the burden of ensuring a complete subscription, the promoter gladly complies. Once the listing is complete, the operator will bide his time, ramp up the prices and offload his shares to the retail public. This is one way of getting an issue subscribed.

Along the way, we've covered many SME companies. But perhaps one of the most egregious cases cropped up when a certain film distributor wanted to raise over a million dollars for his company, which had a combined financial track record of a mere eleven days. To put that into context, imagine a scenario where you start a business today, infuse some capital (mostly cash) and raise over a million dollars from the public in just under two weeks, after you have the red herring prospectus (RHP) approved.

The red herring prospectus is a document submitted by a company (issuer) as part of a public offering of securities (shares). It contains the risks and the potential pitfalls associated with investing in a newly listed company. The only catch here is that SMEs don't actually require the explicit approval of SEBI – India's regulator for the securities market. Instead, the prospectus is approved by the stock exchange and the company gets the go-ahead to list itself on the SME exchange portal. Although the rules for listing have since changed, exchanges don't often flag objections, because of an inherent conflict of interest. Exchanges make money when companies go public, and so, there is little incentive for exchanges to play spoilsport, except when it thinks the regulator could step in.

When we met an insider from one of the exchanges and quizzed him about this, he simply said, 'Nobody reads the RHP (red herring prospectus) for these SMEs. Not the investors, not even the promoter.' *laughs*

Despite the slew of negative stories we've published on SMEs, there were a couple of companies that offered some hope. One company, in particular, had a lot going for it. When we found discrepancies in the balance sheet and called the compliance officer, the CFO personally assured us that the erroneous figure was a misprint, and offered us an elaborate explanation of the company's financials.

It was in the government's interest to promote companies like these when the proposal for an SME stock platform was initiated. So, it is quite unfortunate that it's being hijacked by greedy promoters and fringe financial institutions, which are simply aiming to profit from SMEs by duping the public and getting away with millions scot-free.

We hope both the exchange and SEBI look into this matter with intent, and focus on getting more credible companies on board instead of letting a few bad apples rule the roost. The lax compliance standards for SMEs were put in place to make the listing process hassle-free. However, it is quintessential to balance this act to prevent sham companies from uprooting the integrity of the entire industry. A thorough re-evaluation of compliance standards for SME listings could go a long way in promoting the interests of both SMEs and the Indian retail investor.

WHY ARE TV NEWS STOCK RECOMMENDATIONS A SHAM?

Consider for a moment the method of forecasting. If you had to put a number on a company's future stock price, you'd first have to figure out the company's future earnings potential. To do that, you'd first have to understand the business fundamentals. You'd have to consider the political climate and the macroeconomic variables. You would have to look at threats from the company's biggest competitors. You'd have to analyse potential cost increase if adding new capacity. You would have to sniff out future opportunities and look at the immediate impact on cash flows from threats.

You'd have to assume the cost of borrowing new money and bake in any other numbers that might help project earnings.

Once you are done with these pesky bits, you'd have to assess the current mood of the market. You would have to decide whether the market is paying more or less than what the earnings project. And depending on how long you are looking to hold the stock, you might have to take a stab at assessing the future mood of the market as well. Finally, you toss out all the figures you've so painstakingly calculated, listen to your gut and put out a number that's closest to the market consensus. Basically, you adjust the number so that your forecast doesn't look out of place when compared to other similar projections from your peers. Or if you're looking to stand out, throw a number that's furthest away from the consensus. It's no wonder then that American economist Burton Malkiel famously remarked: 'Financial projection appears to be a science that makes astrology look respectable.'

And look, most experts you see on TV don't even do this. Instead, they offer daily projections based on charts and other technical indicators. In fact, the earliest example of this is from 1949, when an Indian author Fakir Chandra Dutt penned down a rather elaborate exposition on predicting the movement of a stock using astrological principles in his book *Market Forecasting*. He wrote: ' The astrological laws have stood the test of proof and anyone who cares to study the subject with an open mind will find that is he dealing with immutable laws, not fanciful imaginings... The chief aim of the present work is to show that the same laws of the planetary influence can be equally employed in forecasting the rise and fall in prices of commodities, stocks and shares.'

While today's anchors no longer rely on planets, they do rely on a cocktail of other indicators to determine the future price of a stock. They believe that price patterns repeat themselves – that stock behaviour is predictable because humans react to market events with remarkable consistency. They will argue that the new methods are, in fact, an exact science. And despite all academic evidence pointing to the contrary, you'll find that there is considerable support within the trading community about the methods' efficacy. So we won't comment on the merits of such an exercise.

However, what we will comment on is this: The anchors who dabble in such things have a penchant for making bold predictions with absolute conviction. They don't ask you to exercise restraint. Instead, they act as cheerleaders, and urge you to trade based on their speculative bets, whilst not admitting that they are simply hypothesizing. Even Fakir Chandra Dutt had the prescience to call it out for what it is – speculation. He wrote: 'The lookout for the lowest fall and the highest rise [in stock price] is dangerous and should be avoided, for, thereby the speculator generally gets the worse business. Also one should never speculate with all the money he can command but shall lay out a separate fund for speculation.'

And bear in mind, there is nothing wrong in offering an unbiased analysis. In fact, on most occasions, it helps the average retail investor to avoid booby traps, by aiding in their understanding of the business and enabling them to make qualified bets. There are many good advisors who do this, and there are several TV anchors who do a stellar job of reporting on news events and business fundamentals. More power to these folks.

But if you're a TV personality who frequents popular channels and are prodding unsuspecting viewers to buy or sell stocks without intimating them about the uncertainty involved, then you're deceiving them, plain and simple. So, if you're making predictions about the future, then you must address the elephant in the room: How sure are you about your own predictions? If you are not, then why peddle the nonsense to hundreds and thousands of gullible viewers? And why do TV networks extend these people a platform without inquiring about their track record?

When you want to find out whether someone is a good batsman, you look at their batting average. When you want to know whether someone is a good striker, you look at their goal-scoring record. However, a peculiar quirk about this industry is that you could be a market expert without ever managing money or boasting a good track record. You could be off by a country mile with your predictions and nobody would bat an eyelid. In fact, when researchers at the MIT looked at some one-year forecasts from analysts and market experts in the US, they found an average annual error rate of 31% over a five-year period. Which leads us to believe that these experts are consistent alright, but they are consistently off the mark.

It's even more damning when they engage in profiteering from their celebrity status by buying stocks, and dumping them soon after unsuspecting retail investors have followed their call. It's preposterous. The only way this will ever go away is when news channels ask these experts to tone down their rhetoric. For instance, terms such as 'Diwali pataka stocks, Santa rally, muhurtam gains, multibagger picks' need to stop. Granted, many viewers binge on this stuff. But that doesn't make it right. We know this because we wrote about stocks too. In fact, if there's one criticism that we often received during our time at Finception (the blog we ran when we had first started out), it was that we never offered a target price, that we lacked conviction and never recommended stocks.

But the fact of the matter is that even if we did recommend stocks and offered a target price, it would at best be a well-meaning guess and not much more. It would only perpetuate a pernicious illusion that the future is more 'knowable' than it actually is. No amount of financial acrobatics will ever yield consistently accurate projections, and no model will ever produce a perpetual streak of world-beating returns. So despite what other people might tell you, the only way to make big money in the market is to make a bet and pray for divine intervention. If you still harbour illusions about taming uncertainty, then we pray that the odds forever side with you. But if there's one thing that's certain in life, it's that Lady Luck owes no allegiance, for she dances on the annals of victory and broken dreams with equal fervour.

So if the news channels don't stop, maybe the onus is on you.

WHY DO PEOPLE REALLY BUY THE DIP?

In 1924, American author Henry Howard Harper compiled a stunning book called *The Psychology of Speculation*. In one of the chapters, he wrote: 'The individual who trades or invests in stocks will do well to keep away from the stock ticker; for the victim of "tickeritis" is no more capable of reasonable and self-composed action than one who is in the delirium of typhoid fever. The gyroscopic action of the prices recorded on the ticker tape produces a sort of mental intoxication, which foreshortens the vision by involuntary subordination to momentary influences. It also produces on some minds an effect somewhat similar to that which one feels after standing for a considerable time intently watching the water as it flows over the Niagara Falls. Dozens of people, without suicidal intentions, have been drawn into the current and dashed on the rocks below. And thousands daily are influenced by the stock ticker to commit the most fatuous blunders.'

For the uninitiated, a ticker tape is an instrument used to transmit stock price information over telegraph lines, in which a machine churned out thin strips of paper, with stock price information scribbled all over it. People used these tapes as price guides to trade and invest. And while the physical tapes no longer exist, we still have simulated ticker displays plastered on news websites and trading terminals.

But more importantly, almost a hundred years on, we still have people making the most terrible errors based on monetary price fluctuations. Look around you – people are trading speculative assets like compulsive gamblers. They are buying the dip and throwing all caution to the wind. They're foregoing the most important maxim – 'You can't build wealth if you can't conserve capital.' And if you're making irrational decisions driven by the fear of missing out, perhaps it's time to sit back and take a deep breath.

But, let's suppose you already recognize some of these traits within you. Maybe you're trying hard to be a more astute investor/trader, but failing at it because you don't know how to negate these compulsive behaviours. What do you do about them?

Well, perhaps it makes sense to look at them as habits. Habits that don't particularly bode well for you.

As Charles Duhigg describes in his book *The Power of Habit*: 'Habits are powerful but delicate. They can emerge outside our consciousness or can be deliberately designed. They often occur without our permission, but can be reshaped by fiddling with their parts. They shape our lives far more than we realize – they are so strong, in fact, that they cause our brain to cling to them at the exclusion of all else, including common sense.'

So if you have bad habits driving your behaviour, then it will almost inevitably lead to bad outcomes. But it doesn't have to be this way. Most investors double down on their bets because there is a specific habit loop triggering this reaction. Perhaps, a stock alert tips you off about a price drop. A routine then kicks in. You open your investment app, feel restless and twitch after seeing your stocks in the red. In some cases, what follows is a reckless reaction – a trigger response where you start buying the dip.

This is why most people fail to conserve capital. They've delegated decision-making to a part of the brain that doesn't do a lot of thinking. As Duhigg further writes in his book: 'This process in which the brain converts a sequence of actions into an automatic routine is known as chunking and it's at the root of how habits form. There are dozens – if not hundreds – of behavioral chunks that we rely on every day. Some are simple: You automatically put toothpaste on your toothbrush before sticking it in your mouth. Some, such as getting dressed or making the kids' lunch, are a little more complex.'

But deep down, they are all the same – automatic routines designed to delegate menial tasks, so that we can focus on the more important tasks. The fact that these routines enable us to mitigate a lot of strenuous brain function helps on some occasions. But when you rely on these primitive responses to make trading decisions, you are doomed.

If you're buying the dip after careful consideration of all the facts involved, more power to you. But that's not what most people do, is it? They simply can't help themselves. And like compulsive gamblers, they throw good money after bad, in the hopes of stumbling on ever-lasting riches.

You have to break the habit loop

Identify your cues. Know what's triggering the anxiety and the thoughtless response. Once you've done this bit, you can effectively begin the process of change. It can be hard at first but perseverance will pay off. The next time you see a news article or an investment update, mute them both. Get ahead of the game. If you find yourself opening your investment app, make a note of it, then write down what you would do the next time you have a similar urge. It helps. You have to find dopamine hits elsewhere. Talk to your friends who don't induce the fear of missing out. Break the cues, break the rewards, break the routine. Replace them with something else and we promise you'll start making progress.

HOW CAN YOU BE A RATIONAL INVESTOR?

Let's consider a thought experiment. Imagine you are sitting in a classroom, where the professor shows you a small yellow pouch. The pouch is rather plain but then he spices it up. He tells you there is a chance that something valuable might be inside it, but there's also a possibility that there is nothing. He offers the entire class– you and your fellow classmates – a chance to buy it from him. What would you do? What sum would you be comfortable paying for this pouch?

Do you have an answer? Good.

Let's spice this up a little more. Imagine

the professor is a Harvard alumna and is now teaching a course on Introductory Finance at MIT. Do you want to change your initial bid in the face of this new information? Yes? No?

How about we take it one step further. Imagine your fellow classmate, someone you know and who has taken this course earlier, suddenly bids $1,000 out of the blue? What would you do then? Would you bid higher in light of this new development?

Wisdom of crowds or the madness of mobs?

I borrowed the aforementioned case study from a course on edX, where a professor ran the experiment at a live setting. It begins with a girl (who happened to have previously taken his course) who wins the bag after a few rounds of bidding, taking the price to about $80. She then ends up finding out that the bag contained an Apple watch, a product retailing for about $280. Considering the girl had already taken the course, it's likely she knew something about the professor that nobody else did. It's also possible that other students were making their own calculations. Maybe someone assessed that a tenured professor from Harvard would never put an empty bag in front of his students. It's even possible that someone else was simply reacting to a competitor's bid, or maybe a combination of all these forces pushed the price to $80. Although the actual value of the bag was considerably higher than the price attributed by the 'market', the professor argued that the wisdom of the crowds helped them in deciding the price based on all the information available to them. But is the collective wisdom of the crowds always rational?

Consider the bidding had gone up to $10,000, and college-going students paying that hefty sum for a bag whose contents are unknown. Unless they are all related to Bill Gates, it's unlikely they should be bidding anywhere close to that sum. This is because a rational investor makes his decision based on a prudent analysis of the risks and rewards associated with the game. Irrespective of what's in the bag, a rational investor would have bid a sum that's insignificant compared to his net worth, because of the paucity of information available. If a college student bid $5, it would probably make sense, but by bidding $10,000 a student would have violated the basic covenant of prioritizing risk mitigation over maximizing rewards. But what if the bidding involved a bunch of billionaire hedge fund managers. Would a $10,000 bid be justified then? No, because it's highly unlikely a professor would be giving away a $10,000 bag in an experiment. Even if you are worth a billion dollars, a rational decision must be premised on the maximum reward you can potentially reap from the game. However, more often than not, investors forgo this age-old maxim in the pursuit of extravagant riches. The wisdom of crowds can quickly degenerate into the madness of mobs when rational investors come face to face with their most formidable nemesis – their mind.

My bias, my folly

Although most people like to believe that

irrational exuberance is a product of colossal events, it's not. Instead, it's a by-product of systemic bias creeping into the minds of individual investors. The bias can spread by way of a psychological contagion pretty quickly if certain conditions are met. Consider, for example, a story we covered (in 2019) on the real-estate bubble. We received a barrage of comments from a range of exuberant readers – both well-wishers and critics alike. While we are extremely grateful to everyone who wrote to us, we did observe a rather interesting pattern. The fiercest critics were almost always people who were financially involved in real estate, either directly or indirectly. This, however, was expected. Once you build an investment hypothesis, you are more likely to search, interpret, recall or favour information in a way that confirms your pre-existing belief. Behavioural psychologists call this 'confirmation bias', and because our article did not lend credence to the critics' investment hypothesis, they were more inclined to pick holes in our theory. This sort of thinking can often have devastating consequences, because it gives investors a false sense of infallibility, and prevents them from thinking clearly. In the process, they are unable to adequately assess the risks associated with their investment. To better understand the source of this psychological discomfort, let's look at their arguments.

Most people who were extremely critical about our story had one main contention – our analysis was limited to a macroanalysis of the real estate sector, when in fact a more prudent analysis would have involved an exposition of individual micro markets. The argument was this: real estate markets don't behave like one big correlated entity, that is, home prices in Delhi could be falling whilst prices in Mumbai could be on a perpetual rise. If you're living in Mumbai, real estate investments would seem like a pretty good bet. And so, the argument was that any nationwide analysis is useless because markets in Mumbai, Bengaluru, Delhi etc. all behave differently. While this seems like a pretty reasonable argument, it's one of the many logical fallacies that undermine the process of seeking a more definitive understanding of the subject.

False dilemmas

In the above case, the investor reduces the argument to a simple dichotomy, that is, either you do a micro-market analysis or you're wrong. This line of reasoning fails because it limits the options to two, when there are in fact more options to choose from. The real estate industry is connected to the economy in more ways than one. Imagine a developer operating in both Delhi and Bengaluru at the same time. If he experiences stress in Delhi, it's likely to spill over to his assets in Bengaluru as well. This could be further compounded by a funding crunch rising out of a major weakness in the banking industry, in which case the micro markets no longer behave as if they are uncorrelated. Instead, they exhibit high levels of correlation, which is why we see housing bubbles emanating at the macro level affect multiple prongs of a country's economic system.

This is in no way a suggestion that any micro market analysis is futile. A more nuanced analysis is almost always premised on smaller markets operating in different cities. It's also quite possible that the real estate markets could correct themselves without ever breaking down completely. Banks could figure out a way to wriggle out of a funding crunch without ever suffering losses, and the real estate industry could have multiple exit options. But the larger point here is that a plurality of ideas helps stave off bias. Instead of simply sticking to just two options, a gamut of ideas can help investors better understand the sector and further refine their hypothesis. Behavioural psychologists have a name for such people – foxes.

Hedgehogs and foxes

'The fox knows many things, but the hedgehog knows one big thing.'— Archilochus, Greek poet.

In his seminal essay on political forecasting, *Expert Political Judgment* (2006), Philip Tetlock dissects the difference between two personality types – hedgehogs and foxes.

According to him, many political pundits are

hedgehogs, or people who are psychologically biased to be specialists. They often make bombastic claims about future events and characterize them using definite narrow outcomes, without considering the possibility of other sideline events that could affect these outcomes.

Foxes, on the other hand, are more conservative with their predictions. They seek to know a little about a lot of different things. Often, they borrow from a range of ideas and form a more nuanced opinion, which is qualified by multiple if's and but's.

In a bid to critically analyse the efficacy of predictions from both sides (hedgehogs and foxes), Tetlock studied the reliability of their predictions over a period of eighteen years to see who had a better chance at success. He analysed the predictions of over 100 experts and found that the more confident the experts (hedgehogs) were about their predictions, the less accurate they were as compared to random guesses.

Tetlock's research showed that self-proclaimed experts who are overly confident about their analysis are often less reliable in terms of predicting what will happen in the future, even though they might look and sound good. On the other hand, those who were more comfortable questioning and synthesizing multiple choices and stuck to a broad range of outcomes had a visible advantage. The bottom line is – an expert who offers you a long-winded explanation and bores you with an array of 'howevers', is probably right about what's going to happen.

Point of interest – Ask yourself what personality type are you. Be honest :)

Rationalizing man

Tetlock also made another pertinent observation. When the self-proclaimed experts were confronted with evidence of their failed prediction, they would immediately attribute the cause of failure to external factors. Instead of saying, 'I had the wrong theory', the experts would declare, 'It almost went my way', or 'It was the right mistake to make under the circumstances', or 'I'll be proved right later'. In an attempt to reduce the psychological discomfort (cognitive dissonance) of holding contradictory beliefs, people often choose to rationalize their prediction using flimsy accounts of the past. The rational man (one who acts with reason and logic) quickly devolves into the rationalizing man (who defends and justifies himself).

Take, for example, the classic case of cognitive dissonance described in the novel *When Prophecy Fails*. A doomsday cult leader makes a prediction that the world would end for good when aliens start invading the planet. However, despite waiting for a considerable time, the doomsday prophecy failed to materialize. This would have been the ideal condition for the cult's followers to reevaluate the hypothesis and abandon the group and the leader altogether. But that did not happen. Instead, the members of the cult rationalized that the world had been saved by the strength of their faith and continued to trudge along. But, it's never a good idea to rationalize bad decisions, and investors found this out the hard way when the global economy crashed in an almost catastrophic fashion, in 2008.

A case study

In his bestselling novel *The Signal and the Noise*, Nate Silver carefully lays out an exposition of the greatest predictive blunder that ultimately gave way to the financial crisis of 2008.

According to him, one of the primary culprits that was never fully brought to book were the rating agencies. The agencies were responsible for assessing the likelihood of trillions of dollars in mortgage-backed securities going into default. A simple example of a mortgage-backed security is a house loan, and the likelihood of a salaried well-to-do homeowner defaulting on his payment is almost negligible. But greedy brokers backed by Wall Street capitalists found a way to corrupt the system. They started disbursing home loans to increasingly shady (also gullible) people (those with no jobs or no steady income), in the hope of making an extra buck. To make it appealing to investors, they put the good loans and the not-so-good loans together, in a special type of security called the 'collateralized debt obligation' or a CDO.

The hope was that if the mixing was done well enough, the diversification would protect the CDO from going bust, that is, even if some homeowners default, the good homeowners would ensure that the CDO survives. Rating agencies whose income largely came from investment banks were in full agreement, and gladly rated these CDOs as AAA – the gold standard for any asset. For instance, Standard & Poor's, one of the largest rating agencies, told investors that when it rated a particular CDO AAA, there was only a 0.12% probability (about 1 in 850) that it would fail to pay out over the next five years.

By the end of it, however, around 28% of the AAA-rated CDOs went bust. This was an error of epic proportions and it all began with a systemic bias creeping in at the top level. For one, the rating agencies, including some new-age economists, were beginning to think that the wisdom of the crowds had finally matured to a point where catastrophes were being relegated to relics of the past. When someone would point out anything to the contrary, they would immediately be sidelined under the pretext that they were some sort of doomsday conspiracy theorists. In 2005, when Raghuram Rajan presented a paper on the risks associated with CDOs and other complex financial instruments, he came under persistent attacks for being a Luddite or a person who resists change.

There was another popular belief within the financial community – that the real estate markets were not highly correlated. As Nate Silver points out, 'the belief was that if a carpenter in Cleveland defaults on his mortgage [House Loan], it should have no bearing on whether a dentist in Denver does.' Under this scenario, the risk of losing your bet would be exceptionally small, because a CDO (as we have already noted) is an amalgamation of several housing loans pooled into one happy entity.

However, by 2007, home prices were declining across the board, and yet the rating agencies were selectively cherry-picking information to show that the AAA-rated CDOs were good. Instead of taking stock of the events and rerating these instruments (considering they had no prior experience rating these things), they stuck to their guns. Finally, as the housing crisis peaked and homeowners started defaulting on their payments, it was beginning to seem as if the carpenter in Cleveland was defaulting for the same reasons as the dentist in Denver (higher interests as home prices started tumbling). The rating agencies did try and make some adjustments to their complicated rating models, but all of them were woefully inadequate. By the time the dust settled, the US economy was on the verge of collapse.

Be sane, be rational

When heads of these rating agencies found themselves in the hot seat, they immediately shirked responsibility and claimed to have been unlucky. They rationalized their behaviour by blaming an external contingency – housing prices. Looking back, we know for a fact that this is not true. The rating agencies were aware that prices were on the decline, and in some cases, they were actively predicting the decline, but they were so sure of their models that they did not want to change their original hypothesis. Confirmation bias had given way to denial. The denial further emboldened other frenzied investors. The mad mob baying for everlasting riches found a way to precipitate a crisis like no other, and when the party ended the community rationalized their behaviour suggesting that there was no way anyone could see it coming.

Perhaps the only way, then, to protect yourself from the ills of self-confirming theories and belief systems is to adopt the idea of falsification. Investors should perhaps actively seek to falsify themselves in a bid to better understand their own hypothesis. If you find evidence that contradicts your beliefs, don't scoff at it. Instead, embrace it and see whether you need to abandon or modify some of your assumptions. Scepticism in the game of investing can go a long way in protecting your wealth, and most investors would agree that it is much easier to be rational when your capital is intact.

Fellow readers, are you rational? Think about it.

WHICH STATE HAS THE HIGHEST NUMBER OF INVESTORS?

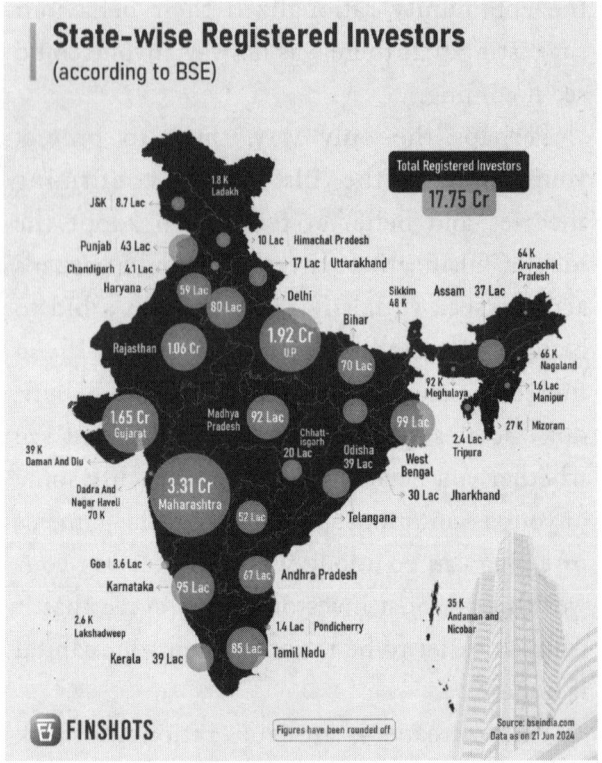

If you are a finance newbie just trying to educate yourself about the ins and outs of the capital markets, you might have thought to yourself: 'What's with all this complex jargon? I'm more confused now than before!'

Well, we are no strangers to how intimidating (and annoying) jargon can be. So, we thought why not simplify it?

Here are some of the most commonly used jargons broken down in a language you'd easily understand:

WHAT IS CAGR?

CAGR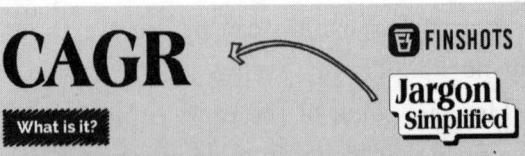

FINSHOTS

Jargon Simplified

What is it?

"How well are my investments doing?"

Everyone wants the answer to that question. And more often than not, we simply calculate the percentage change in value of the investment and are happy when we see a number. We don't consider the time it has taken for the money to grow. For instance, if ₹1 lakh has grown to ₹5 lakhs in 20 years, we say, "Wow, my investment is up by 5x". But we ignore what's the actual yearly return.

That's what CAGR or the **Compounded Annual Growth Rate** helps you calculate. It takes into account the time period of your investment and gives you the average yearly return you made.

How to calculate it

$$\text{Absolute Growth Rate} = \frac{\text{Ending Value of an Investment} - \text{Initial Value of an Investment}}{\text{Initial Value of an Investment}} \times 100$$

$$\text{CAGR} = \left[\left(\frac{\text{Ending Value of an Investment}}{\text{Initial Value of an Investment}}\right)^{1/n} - 1\right] \times 100 \quad \text{*n = Number of years}$$

Here's an example

20 years ago, Popeye invested ₹1,00,000 in a company that grew organic spinach. The company's valuation rose and so did his investment. It's now worth ₹5,00,000. Here's how much Popeye's investment grew in percentage terms.

$$\text{Absolute Growth Rate} = \frac{5,00,000 - 1,00,000}{1,00,000} \times 100 = 400\% \text{ (in total)}$$

$$\text{CAGR} = \left[\left(\frac{5,00,000}{1,00,000}\right)^{1/20} - 1\right] \times 100 = 8.4\% \text{ (every year)}$$

WHAT IS P/E RATIO?

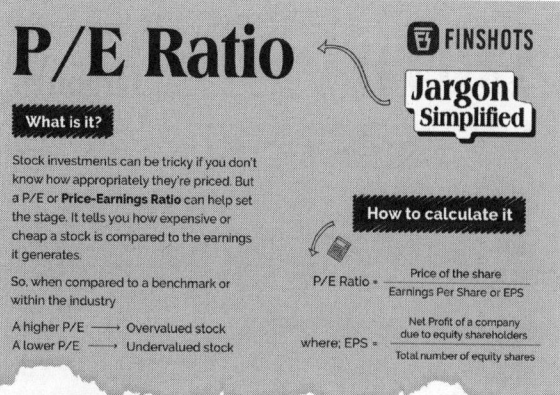

Here's an example

Charlie Brown wants to invest in tech stocks—

Average P/E for tech company stocks:	26
P/Es of the companies he's shortlisted:	
Snoopy Tech —	22
Woodstock Tech —	30

This means that:

- Investors are willing to pay ₹22 and ₹30 for each rupee that Snoopy and Woodstock make respectively.
- Snoopy's stock is cheaper + undervalued amongst its industry peers.
- But a cheap P/E doesn't necessarily make it a great buy. Investors may not believe in its future prospects.

So Charlie will have to research other metrics beyond P/E.

WHAT IS EBITDA?

EBITDA

Imagine that you started a company a year ago. You now want to check your business' operating efficiency and its ability to generate a core profit. How would you do it? Well, you could use EBITDA.

E **Earnings** The revenue left after your company subtracts operating expenses from operating income.

B **Before**

I **Interest** The money your company pays for its debts.

T **Tax** Amounts paid via direct taxes. Indirect taxes like GST or customs aren't considered.

D **Depreciation** Reduction in the value of your company's physical assets.

A **Amortization** Reduction in the value of your company's intangible assets such as trademarks, copyrights, etc.

Here's an example

Extract from **Barbeque Nation's** financials for the first 3 months (Q1) of FY24:

	(₹ in millions)
Revenue from operations	3,239
Other Income	9
Total Revenue	**3,248**
Cost of food and beverages	1,166
Employee expenses	717
Occupancy and other expenses	888
EBITDA	**476**
Finance costs	187
Depreciation & Amortization	375
Exceptional items*	(31)
Profit Before Tax	**(55)**
Tax expense/Benefits#	(14)
Profit/(Loss) After Tax	**(41)**

How to calculate it

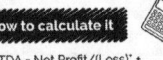

EBITDA = Net Profit/(Loss)* + Interest + Taxes + Depreciation + Amortization

*Your company's earnings after deducting all operating, interest and tax expenses.

* Exceptional items - Huge expenses or incomes that don't occur routinely during the year.

\# This can arise due to accounting adjustments of assets, liabilities, past taxes and other allowances.

So, if you apply the EBITDA formula to Barbeque Nation's Net Profit or Profit After Tax and calculate backwards, you'll arrive at its EBITDA.

WHAT IS CALL OPTION?

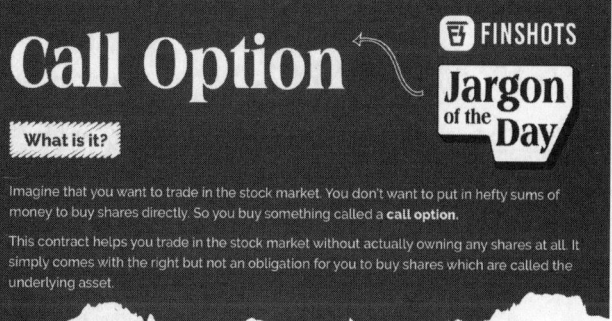

Here's an example

Shares of Hey Ltd are trading at ₹100 each. You're very optimistic about its prospects but if you want to buy 1,000 shares, it'll cost you ₹1,00,000. But you don't have that kind of money.

So you look to buy a call option. All you have to do is pay a small premium — say ₹10,000 and you can buy 1 lot of Hey Ltd which contains 1,000 shares. A month later, you find that the price has risen to ₹120. So you exercise your right and buy the shares at the predetermined price of ₹100. Then you quickly sell them in the market for ₹120.

You make:

(₹120-₹100) x 1000 shares	₹20,000
Less: Premium Paid	₹10,000
Profit	₹10,000

But what if the price had dropped to ₹80?

You're under no obligation to buy at the predetermined price of ₹100. You can simply ignore the contract. Your loss is limited to the premium you paid.

Meanwhile, if you had bought 1,000 shares directly at ₹100 and the price dropped to ₹80, you'd have lost ₹20,000.

Subscribe to finshots.in

WHAT IS PUT OPTION?

Put Option

What is it?

Let's say you're a stock market trader who's quite pessimistic about the near-term prospects of a company. You obviously won't buy the shares just to watch your money evaporate. But what if you could profit from the fall in price? That would be great, no?

So you decide to participate in something called a put option. This is a simple contract where you pay a fee or a premium and get the right, but not the obligation, to sell shares at a predetermined price.

Here's an example

Shares of Yay Ltd are trading at ₹100 each. You believe the stock could fall in value over the next month. So you buy a **put option.**

You pay a small premium – say ₹10,000 and you get the right to sell 1 lot of Yay Ltd at its prevailing price. And 1 lot contains 1,000 shares. True to your bet, the price of Yay Ltd soon falls to ₹80. So you exercise the put option and sell 1 lot of Yay Ltd at the predetermined price of ₹100.

But since you sold these shares at ₹100 without owning them in the first place, you might now need to enter into an opposite transaction and buy those shares at ₹80 to even it out.

You make:

(₹100-₹80) x 1000 shares	₹20,000
Less: Premium Paid	₹10,000
Profit	₹10,000

But what if the price had risen to ₹120?

You're under no obligation to exercise the put option. You can ignore the contract and your loss is limited to the premium you paid.

WHAT ARE FORWARDS AND FUTURES?

Forwards & Futures

What is it?

Forward contracts help you freeze the price of commodities you want to buy or sell in the future and hedge yourself from losses. Similar contracts that are tradeable on commodity exchanges are called **futures contracts**

Let's understand this with an example

Freddy runs a pancake shop. He feels that inflation could drive up flour prices in a few weeks. So he enters into a contract to buy 10 kilos of flour at ₹100 per kilo after a fortnight from Teddy.

After a fortnight, if the flour price -

↑ to ₹120/kg - Freddy saves ₹200 (or ₹20/kg).
↓ to ₹80/kg - Teddy gains ₹200.

But forwards can be risky if either party defaults on their contracts. So they can enter into something called a futures contract.

The only difference?
They
- are regulated.
- are tradable on a commodity exchange.
- don't involve the delivery of underlying assets like forwards.

Rather, Freddy and Teddy would interact with an intermediary called the clearing house. Both must deposit sufficient funds called margins with this entity, from where their profits and losses get adjusted.

WHAT IS BLUE CHIP STOCK?

Blue Chip Stock

What is it?

It's a term used to describe stocks of companies that have acquired their consumers' trust & perform well even in tough market conditions.

It was coined in 1923 by Oliver Gingold, a Dow Jones employee who used it to describe stocks trading at $200 or more per share. He was probably inspired by a game of poker, where blue gambling chips represent the highest value on the table.

But how do I know if a stock is a Blue Chip Stock?

- It has a significant market capitalisation (share price x total no. of shares of the company), ideally ≥ ₹20,000 crores although there's no hard & fast rule
- Its products/services have a large market share
- It has a strong financial position & offers steady profits/dividends to its shareholders
- It enjoys great brand value & has an impressive track record of business performance
- It's generally a part of stock market indices like the NIFTY 50 or SENSEX

Here are some examples

There isn't a formal list of blue chip stocks in the market but here are some names synonymous with the term

Disclaimer: This is just an explainer, so please don't take it as investment advice.

WHAT IS VIX?

VIX (Volatility Index) — FINSHOTS — Jargon Simplified

What is it?

Ever wondered how analysts predict future stock market uncertainties/volatilities? Well, they look at something called the VIX or Volatility Index. It's simply a measure of the stock market's expectation of uncertainties in the near future or the next 30 days.

How is it calculated

VIX uses a complicated formula based on the Black Scholes model, which is used to price derivative financial instruments, particularly options.

> A contract that helps you trade in the stock market without actually owning any shares at all. It comes with the right but not an obligation for you to buy/sell shares or indexes like SENSEX, NIFTY 50, etc. (called the underlying asset)

Simply put, VIX looks at the time remaining until an option contract's expiry, the interest rate offered by safe investments like govt. bonds for the same period and the intensity of the volatility.

Good to know

- VIX is based on S&P 500 Index Options. But India VIX is based on the prices of NIFTY options contracts.
- If Price of VIX↑, then Price of Indexes like SENSEX/NIFTY ↓
- Sometimes VIX can go in the same direction as the NIFTY. For eg; stock markets rise in anticipation of election results, but VIX rises too because the market can also be very uncertain.
- VIX goes up before major events like elections. As of 7 May, 2024 India VIX stood at 17, the highest since 30 Jan, 2024.
- VIX is also called fear index/fear gauge.

WHAT ARE GROWTH STOCKS AND VALUE STOCKS?

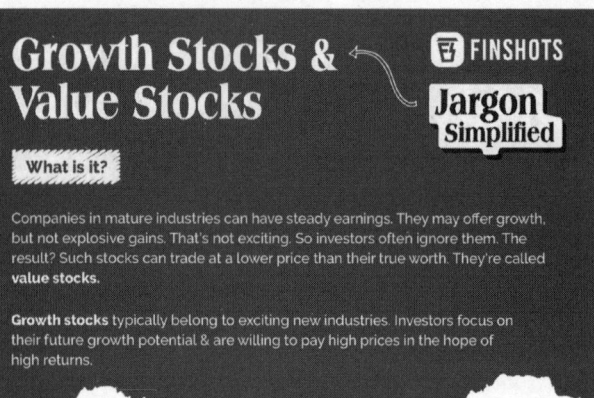

Growth Stocks & Value Stocks

FINSHOTS

Jargon Simplified

What is it?

Companies in mature industries can have steady earnings. They may offer growth, but not explosive gains. That's not exciting. So investors often ignore them. The result? Such stocks can trade at a lower price than their true worth. They're called **value stocks.**

Growth stocks typically belong to exciting new industries. Investors focus on their future growth potential & are willing to pay high prices in the hope of high returns.

Let's understand this with an example

Jon is an analyst. Here's what his calculations about an Oil & Gas company stock suggest

True Worth of the stock — ₹100
Market Price — ₹70

Jon thinks that investors have ignored this trustworthy company since renewable energy is all the buzz now. But he believes that the world still needs a lot of oil & sees **value** in the stock.

Jane, another analyst believes that renewable energy is the future. So she decides to buy an EV company's stock. It may not generate a lot of profits today, but will in the future. Many other analysts think like her too. So, the stock may be pricey because they're all willing to pay a premium for this future **growth**.

WHAT IS UPPER AND LOWER CIRCUIT?

Upper and Lower Circuit

FINSHOTS

What is it?

Let's assume that you decided to buy a company's stock after careful research. But many other investors like you rushed to buy it too. The demand peaked so much that it hit a new high.

But the stock exchange saw this coming and fixed an upper price limit. That's the **Upper Circuit.** On the flip side, if some bad news affecting this stock's business suddenly breaks out, investors might panic and start selling it. But the stock exchange would have also set a lower limit called the **Lower Circuit.**

So, a stock's price can only move between this price band during the day. It protects investors from extreme volatility.

How to calculate it

Market regulator SEBI pre-decides a daily price range for a stock. This depends on the previous day's closing price.

For instance, if a stock has a circuit limit of 5% and it closed at ₹100 yesterday. It can only shoot up or dip by ₹5 today. So the price band is ₹95-₹105.

But different stocks can have different limits which can be 2%, 5%, 10% or even 20%.

Here's an example

Dips/Rise in Jio Financial Services' Stock Price

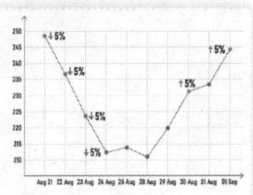

Note: The stock listed on the NSE on 21 Aug and hit its lower circuit from its listing price of ₹262.00.

● Lower Circuit
● Upper Circuit

BUSINESS

WHAT ARE TAX HAVENS AND WHY DO THEY EXIST?

According to an article published in the *International Consortium of Investigative Journalists*, 'There is no universal definition, but tax havens, or offshore financial centres, are generally countries or places with low or no corporate taxes that allow outsiders to easily set up businesses there. Tax havens also typically limit public disclosure about companies and their owners. Because information can be hard to extract, tax havens are sometimes also called secrecy jurisdictions.'

These jurisdictions can be quite enticing if you are looking to stash money abroad. But not all funds are created equal and not everybody has the same objective.

For starters, you have money held by rich people – income that's routed to off-shore financial centres and isn't taxed . This money could be legal income made through honest work or illicit wealth amassed using criminal activities. And while using an offshore account isn't illegal per se, most people don't declare this information to local tax authorities in a bid to save money. And that, believe it or not, is illegal. By some estimates, 'the global rich held in 2007 approximately $12 trillion of their wealth in tax havens.'

That's quite a lot of money.

But there is another category – tax savings of multinational corporations, who use tax havens to pay little or no taxes in countries where they operate. According to one report, countries lose $245 billion each year to corporate tax abuse. And it's extremely hard to prevent this, because most of it is actually legal. As one report notes:

'The tax avoidance mechanisms of multinationals is even more challenging than recovering the money hidden by individuals. The reason is that unlike the practices of individual tax cheats, what multinationals are doing often is legal. The law as it presently stands in many countries allows them to incorporate offshore in tax havens with no or only low taxes. The result has been trillions of dollars in savings for the companies. Perhaps the most unjust aspect of this practice is that by increasing profits through tax avoidance, multinationals are increasing the value of their stock. This amounts to taxpayers subsidizing, through lost taxes, these companies' shareholders.'

It's like honest taxpayers filling the coffers of corporations that are already worth trillions of dollars. And while it's true that high-income countries lose more tax revenue in absolute numbers, the brunt of the burden is borne by developing countries, who don't make a lot in tax revenue to begin with. For instance, in India, while only 2.2% of the country's voting population pay income tax, it is still the primary source of revenue for the government.

So it's imperative to ask – how on earth are

companies and individuals still getting away with this?

Well, look. You're probably thinking about pinning the blame on Swiss Banks and secretive laws that protect the identity of some of these individuals and corporations. But we are not going to talk about them. Instead, we'll look at another major antagonist – the United Kingdom. Or more specifically, the United Kingdom's spider web of overseas territories and crown dependencies. Think, Cayman Islands, or the British Virgin Islands. In fact, Britain has fourteen overseas territories, and seven of them are generally thought of as tax havens.

But why did offshore banking flourish in these areas? How did these tiny island states, with a combined population of 2,50,000, do this much damage?

Well, that's a long story. But let us try and summarize it for you.

Soon after World War II, the British Empire was on the decline. Having lost their major colonies, they were trying to hold on to the last vestiges of power. And then, the Egyptian president Abdel Nasser landed a body blow to them by nationalizing the Suez Canal. Assuming full control of the vital trade route, he was in a position to choke off a critical supply line. Bear in mind that the canal was owned and operated by Britain and France, until the Egyptians took over in July 1956. And since this was a strategic asset for both countries, they couldn't simply watch from the sidelines. So when Israel invaded Egypt in October of the same year, Britain and France saw an opportunity to overthrow the president and take control of the canal. However, after pressure from the US and the UN began to mount, all three invaders were forced to call off the invasion and retreat. For Britain, this meant losing control of the Suez permanently, and investors were contemplating if the country was headed towards financial ruin.

Some investors who foresaw this eventuality started exchanging British currency for something they thought was valuable. And as the Pound lost its sheen, Britain's central bank was forced into action. They immediately halted domestic banks from lending money to overseas borrowers. The hope was that they could stem the flow of currency out of the country, which would help keep a leash on the value of the Pound. However, bankers were upset about losing business and a compromise was sought. But the compromise was quite ridiculous.

The central bank stipulated that foreign lending could continue so long as the transactions transpired in non-sterling currency. In other words, a currency that wasn't the British Pound. Second, the central bank mandated that both lenders and borrowers had to reside outside the UK. Where else could they be based, you ask? Well, anywhere.

As one report in the BBC notes:

'They [the central bank] simply deemed certain transactions as not taking place in the UK. Where did the transactions take place for regulatory purposes? Nowhere.'

But since the banks needed an address, they simply chose the British Overseas Territories. And while they were at it, they figured out that it was an excellent way to circumvent key regulations and to borrow/lend billions without any oversight from the government. Also, local authorities in the overseas territories deliberately designed regulations to make the process of setting up accounts to borrow or lend money more seamless. And offshore banking took off in a massive way. Today, these territories are responsible for tax losses of some $160 billion each year. And while the British government continues to maintain innocence, by declaring that these territories are individual self-governing states, it isn't a very sustainable proposition. Key government officials in the territories are appointed by the British Crown, and even their laws are approved in London. So the UK does hold a significant influence in these territories.

The bottom line is that unless Britain does something about this, beyond issuing hollow statements, we will continue to see the rich getting richer and the poor getting fleeced.

And tax havens?

Well, they'll just continue to thrive.

WHAT ARE THE BRANDS THAT HAVE HELPED BUILD INDIA?

Godrej & Boyce

You've probably heard of Godrej Industries, makers of Cinthol soap and Good Knight mosquito repellent. But that's not what made them famous. Their claim to fame are the sturdy, grey-coloured almirahs – the ubiquitous product that has been a staple of middle-income Indian households since the 1920s.

Back in the day, parents gave away an almirah as a wedding present! In the 1980s, the company even ran ads to further drive home this point – that a Godrej cupboard could build an everlasting bond between a husband and wife. They were an integral part of many Indian families, including mine.

But, before the success of the almirahs, the company was known as Godrej & Boyce. And you could argue that it was inextricably linked with India's journey as a newly independent nation.

Okay, in 1952, as India was gearing up for its first-ever elections, it needed 12.83 lakh ballot boxes. And they had to be sturdy and tamper-proof.

Guess who stepped up to the plate?

Godrej & Boyce.

The company had already built an impressive resume manufacturing locks and safes, and they immediately stood up to the lofty challenge. According to the then plant manager, K.R. Thanewalla, workers slogged it out from 7 am to 12 am every day, for nearly four months, to meet the target.

Needless to say, Godrej did it. The ballot boxes were a resounding success. They were in use until the 1960s.

> **Fun fact:** If all the ballot boxes were placed on top of each other, it would go as high as 36 Mount Everests.

Chemical, Industrial and Pharmaceutical Laboratories (Cipla)

Though India is a pharmaceutical giant today, the industry wasn't as promising back in the day.

In fact, the origins of India's market leadership can be traced back to the Independence era. Until 1947, Western multinational corporations controlled India's pharmaceutical industry, holding almost 99% of the patents. Since patent laws fully protected the drugs made by the Western corporations, they had no competition, and could price their products the way they deemed fit. Unfortunately, it came at the expense of the Indian public as their domestic drug prices were among the highest in the world.

But in the 1970s, the government decided to switch things up. To protect the manufacturing process of making the drugs, they tweaked

India's patent laws. That meant you could copy the end product as long as you found a way to reverse-engineer the process. And since, patent laws' protection of western medicine was done away with, it led to a boom in production.

But wait ... who was instrumental in implementing this change?

Well, you could probably credit Dr Yusuf Hamied – the son of Dr Khwaja Abdul Hamied, who founded the pharmaceutical company Cipla! After finishing his PhD from Cambridge University, Yusuf Hamied returned to join his father's pharmaceutical business, in the 1960s.

But what he saw shocked him. India still upheld the British Patent Law of 1911, which made drugs unaffordable. He then set up the Indian Drug Manufacturers' Association and lobbied the Indian government to change the rules. He succeeded! In 1972, the government introduced new reforms and thus began a glorious new chapter for Indian pharma.

But the story isn't over, yet.

You see, Cipla's contribution didn't begin there. In 1939, three years after setting up Cipla,

Mahatma Gandhi visited Dr K.A. Hamied with a rather peculiar request. At the time, British forces were fighting the Second World War and needed a few life-saving drugs to keep their troops alive. They promised to look favourably on India's Independence demands if they got those all-important medicines. Gandhi wanted Cipla to intervene, and they did, manufacturing vitamin B12 and anti-malarial pills in bulk.

And the rest, as they say, is history.

Amul

Long before Amul stormed on the dairy scene, there was another dairy behemoth – Polson Dairy. Incidentally, the latter too had its roots in Gujarat. In the 1940s, they were the go-to company for dairy products, especially butter, which everyone loved. The consumers even had a soft corner for the blond-haired girl featured in the Polson ads.

But, while the butter was a consumer favourite, it left a bad taste in the mouth of the dairy farmers. All thanks to the company's monopolistic practices.

You see, Polson enjoyed the support of the government, and so the dairy farmers in the region had to sell their milk at throwaway prices. The company pocketed most gains and the farmers weren't being rewarded adequately.

Finally, in 1946, the farmers had had enough. They decided to band together and create a cooperative called the Kaira District Cooperative Milk Producers' Union Limited. Two villages, 250 litres of milk. That's it. That was the beginning. Instead of routing the milk through Polson, they supplied it directly to the folks in Mumbai.

Little did anyone know that this was the beginning of what would become the world's biggest dairy cooperative. A movement led by Dr Verghese Kurien that would transform India from being a milk-deficient country to one of the world's largest milk producers.

Oh, and the famous Amul Girl? It was created in 1966 by Sylvester DaCunha, an advertising executive. And let's just say he may have taken some inspiration from the Polson girl.

WHAT IS THE PRICE OF YOUR ATTENTION?

The internet is an amazing place. It can teach you how to put on eyeliner in four different ways. It can show you videos of a cat pooping on a dog. It can offer you access to a newsletter that breaks down complex financial concepts. Ergo, you always have access to a lot of information – way more than you'll ever be able to process.

While one might be inclined to think most of this information is free, it's not. Granted, you may not be spending actual cash, but you are paying with another currency – your attention.

Consider Facebook.

'Facebook is free and always will be,' is the

company's famous slogan. But that doesn't mean it is not making money. In fact, they are making billions. And to keep making more money than they did the previous year, Facebook needs to convince advertisers to pay top dollar. But that won't happen unless the advertisers are convinced that people will pay attention to them. So, in essence, platforms like Facebook have a big incentive to keep you mindlessly scrolling for hours, because they are literally profiting off your attention.

This is what brands are competing for. This is what social networks are optimizing for.

They do this in several insidious ways. Facebook talks to you like a caring friend – 'What's on your mind?' Instagram uses visuals to make people yearn for a better life. LinkedIn exploits the human need for social acceptance. YouTube and Netflix play the next video or episode before you've even decided to watch it. Snapchat uses daily streaks to compel young people to use it every day.

Moreover, every network uses a combination of elements, such as reactions, emojis, tags, shares, to keep you engaged for as long as possible. Every time you like something, you feel you're supporting someone. Every time someone likes something you've put out in the virtual world, you get an instant dopamine hit. It makes you feel good. It makes you want to experience more of that feeling.

Also, that little red icon that pops up whenever you get a new notification? You see it and immediately want to find out what it contains. It could be something important, you argue. And even if it's not, pressing the button will make it go away. Hell, they even optimize for colour.

Back in the old days, the Facebook notification icon was blue, in keeping with the rest of their design. But that wasn't clickbaity enough. So, they switched to red, and immediately more people began responding to it. It has since been adopted by other social networks. Red is a trigger colour – it's used for emergencies. It compels you to take immediate action, even if there's a chance that you'll be disappointed. Especially if there's a chance that you'll be disappointed.

Because all of this has remarkable similarities to gambling.

The pull to refresh mechanism, where users pull down their mobile screens, pause and wait for new posts to appear, uses the same psychology. It's like a slot machine. You can't be sure what you'll get. Will it be a new picture of your crush or just a blurry family shot of your elderly tuition teacher? Pull down to find out. Not what you wanted? Pull down again.

According to a leaked report, Facebook is even monitoring posts and photos in real-time to get a feel of its users' emotions. It can find out when people feel stressed, defeated, anxious or happy, etc. They can optimize users' feeds accordingly. They share these insights with advertisers, so that they can better understand how to target their audience. Facebook even has information on users' discussions. So now you know why you start seeing ads of gyms the moment you resolve to get fit.

None of this is all that surprising. Social networks clearly have all the incentives in the world to get users to spend more time on their platforms. It's up to the consumers to decide what they should do with the scarce resource that is their attention.

As the famous saying goes, 'If you're not paying for the product, you are the product.'

Except if you are using Finshots. Hehe :P

WHY ARE CEOs OVERPAID AND EMPLOYEES UNDERPAID?

Chief executive officers in private sector companies across India make 137 times more than their median employee. In the IT sector, a CEO's pay is 141 times higher than the median pay. In the pharma sector, we see a multiple of 238 (as of 2022).

Globally too, we see the same story unfold. The CEO-to-worker pay gap has expanded exponentially over the past few decades. During the 1970s, the average CEO in the US made 31 times more than the typical worker. That jumped to 61 times by 1990. By 2020? Well, you better sit down for this – it was a staggering 351 times higher! And some studies show that this burgeoning inequality leads to high attrition, low levels of employee satisfaction and even lower sales.

So policymakers are now deliberating whether to rein in this inequality. Some are considering capping CEO salaries to improve outcomes.

If you're reading this, you will most likely agree with the above assessment, and concede that there's absolutely no reason why CEOs should get paid such obscene amounts of money while employees continue to scrape the bottom of the barrel.

However, this thinking has some flaws. For instance, consider a cricketing analogy. As a batsman, Virat Kohli gets paid disproportionately more than his peers, who try to ply their trade in Ranji cricket. Both cricketers try and hit a ball with a piece of willow, and yet there's a massive gap in pay. In fact, over the years, this inequality has only exacerbated. But if you think about it, you can see why this is happening. Elite cricketers are a step above 'good' cricketers.

And the market for elite cricketers looks very different compared to the market for just 'good' cricketers. There just aren't enough people who can do what Kohli does on a daily basis. And since cricket lovers are willing to pay a premium for quality entertainment, Kohli continues to get paid the big money.

Now some of you will look at this and go –'Well, his performance doesn't really warrant that kind of money. After all, his form isn't great all the time.' And you'd have a point. But then, the market also accounts for this anomaly. If his form deteriorates, he won't be able to pull in the same kind of money from his cricketing pursuits. Somebody will replace him – as people do in a system based on meritocracy. This is what free-market economists believe.

The market for CEOs is tiny. You just don't have enough people who can consistently do what the top professionals do. So it's natural they get paid a sum that reflects their ability. In fact, some studies show that capping CEO salaries can, in fact, have an adverse effect on employee outcomes.

After China imposed pay restrictions on

CEOs of centrally administered state-owned enterprises, the top-level executives simply increased their consumption of perks and siphoned off firm's resources for their own benefit. The performance of these firms also dropped following pay restrictions and affected both hiring decisions and employee pay.

Even simple disclosures about pay ratios can have unintended consequences. For instance, Alex Edmans (Professor of Finance at London Business School) argues: 'A CEO wishing to improve the ratio may outsource low-paid jobs, hire more part-time than full-time workers, or invest in automation rather than labour. She may also raise workers' salaries but slash other benefits.'

So clearly, it's not just as simple as capping CEO salaries or forcing them to improve the 'CEO-to-worker' pay ratio. What we really need is reform, to ensure that CEOs have the right incentive to create value that will help elevate the salaries of everyone, not just their own.

How do we do that? Well, maybe that's a story for a different day.

HOW DID BUSINESSES FORGE AHEAD AFTER PARTITION?

Here's a deep dive into some unusual stories about some very usual brands:

Parle

Dunking a humble biscuit into a cup of morning *chai* is perhaps a part of daily routine for most of us. But that wasn't the case in pre-independent India. The market was dominated by British biscuit brands, such as United Biscuits, Huntly & Palmers and Britannia (a subsidiary of a British company).

But a man called Narottam Mohanlal Chauhan wanted to change that. He wanted a *swadeshi* biscuit.

Along with his brothers, he'd already set up a confectionary brand in 1929 in a small town called Parla in Mumbai's (then Bombay) suburbs. They made orange candies and toffees. And so, they had a fair knowledge of how to run a food business.

And when a biscuit factory was put up for sale in 1938, the brothers decided to snap it up. But since they didn't have biscuit-making experience, Narottam travelled to England to learn the ropes. He returned not just with the art but even the machinery needed to make biscuits.

Their first wheat biscuit emerged the same year – Parle Gluco! Yup, the same biscuit that would go on to become the iconic Parle-G.

But as luck would have it, the Second World War broke out shortly after. Everything was then being rationed. Even the wheat needed for the biscuits. Parle got a limited amount and was told to make the biscuits only for the army. And to produce biscuits for the Indian public, they had to resort to using barley. It tasted horrible. And these are not our words, but what one of the Chauhan descendants said in an interview. They even had to use newspaper as packaging material.

If we put the sequence of events together, it seems as though it was only after the War that Parle could give Indians a taste of the wheat-based glucose biscuits (even though their website makes no mention of this).

But that didn't last long. Because then came Partition and India lost large swathes of its crucial wheat territories of West Punjab (now in Pakistan) and East Pakistan (now Bangladesh). We were left with just about 60% of our wheat supplies.

So, Parle had to hit pause on its Gluco biscuit production. They then put out ads asking people to buy their barley biscuits, instead. Just until the dust settled down.

The rest of course is history. The iconic yellow packaging with the girl emerged in the 1960s, making the product stand out. And today, Parle sells 1.2 million tonnes of biscuits every year. The swadeshi biscuit is now the world's biggest biscuit brand.

Fun fact: If the total number of Parle-G packets produced in a year are placed around the Earth's circumference, they would circle the Earth 192 times.

Hamdard

The year was 1906, when a young Hakim Hafiz Abdul Majeed set up shop in Delhi. He was a practitioner of Unani, an Islamic system of medicine, and he wanted to sell products to cure people's ailments.

But he soon noticed something around him. Delhi's summers were scorching, and it was making people suffer from heatstrokes rather frequently. So he put his head down and got to work to create something that would fix the problem. Something that would help cool the body down. He mixed herbs, such as coriander, chicory, stone flower, mint and khas (a fragrant grass), then added rose petals, some colouring and of course sugar too – the end result was a herbal drink that had a reddish tinge to it.

And people loved it. Its demand soared through the roof, and the bottles quickly flew off the shelves.

This was the beginning of Rooh Afza.

The craze continued for many, many years during the British rule, and the business soon passed on to his sons. But when the Partition of the country was announced, a choice had to be made – should they remain in India or move base to Pakistan?

Well, here's what happened.

Hakim Majeed's younger son Hakim Mohammed Said moved to Pakistan and set up the Hamdard Laboratories in Karachi. His elder son Hakim Abdul Majeed stayed on in India and continued the business under Hamdard Laboratories India.

Basically, Rooh Afza chose to stay undivided.

And even after Bangladesh achieved independence from Pakistan in 1971, the family set up a new entity in the east. And that's the story of how Rooh Afza came to conquer India, Pakistan and Bangladesh.

In fact, today Rooh Afza accounts for over 50% of Hamdard India's sales. Such is the demand that in May 2019, when Rooh Afza was in short supply, its Pakistani arm offered to supply the beverage via the Wagah border.

Quite a unique tryst with the history of India's Partition, no?

Dalda

Ghee, which is made from cow's milk, can be over four times more expensive than edible oil. This has been the norm since time immemorial, even in pre-independent India. So, ghee was reserved only for delicacies and special occasions.

So a Dutch company called Dada decided to cash in on this opportunity. It figured out that it could make something that looked and felt similar to ghee. It was a cheap alternative to the real thing. They called the new product vanaspati ghee and imported it for sale in the country.

Now, Lever Brothers (which eventually came to be called Unilever) saw a big market in this segment as well. In Europe, they'd recently diversified from personal care products to food products, and they probably felt that they could set up a manufacturing facility in India. They soon bought the rights from Dada to manufacture vanaspati on Indian soil and set up the Hindustan Vanaspati Manufacturing Company.

Oh, and the name became Dalda too.

You see, the Dutch company wanted Hindustan Vanaspati to carry its legacy, while the Lever Brothers wanted to stamp their new authority. So they simply inserted the 'L' (for Lever) into the mix and Dada became Dalda. The low-cost alternative soon became a raging success.

But then, what happened during Partition?

Well, initially, there were issues of course. Dalda's distribution took a hit as its wholesalers were caught in violent skirmishes. But as Prakash Tandon, the man who handled Dalda's sales during Partition (and went on to become Hindustan Lever's first Indian chairman), wrote in his memoir that he made a promise to everyone that he would do all he could to help

– keep jobs ready, help exchange their business, homes and Dalda trucks and carts if they were moving across the border.

Over the next few years, the business grew rather slowly. By 1956, Unilever had merged with its subsidiaries, becoming Hindustan Unilever. It even launched an IPO, which meant that Indians could now actually own a piece of the company that made the legendary Dalda or vanaspati ghee products.

But wait…this wasn't strictly an Indian invention, no? And the global behemoth Unilever's might was behind it. So, in the 1950s, Unilever set up shop in Pakistan too, sensing that the palates of the two countries were similar.

And that's how the iconic yellow tin with a green palm tree continued its success story on either side of the border.

But over time, people realized that vanaspati ghee might not actually be as healthy as ghee. So they shifted to refined vegetable oils. Maybe it was the declining sales and market share that made Hindustan Unilever wash its hands of the business by 2003. In India, it sold Dalda to Bunge, an American food brand, who later introduced a line of refined oils. In 2004, it sold the Pakistan business to the Westbury Group, which renamed the company to Dalda Food Products. In 2023, the Pakistani counterpart had even planned to launch the country's biggest-ever IPO by a consumer staples company!

So yeah, that's how Dalda continues its legacy today – as Dalda but under different owners.

THE BIGGEST CRYPTO SCAM IN HISTORY?

In 2016, Ruja Ignatova, a Bulgarian-born German businesswoman, addressed a cheerful crowd at the Wembley Stadium in London.

'OneCoin is on course to becoming the world's biggest cryptocurrency, so everyone can make payments everywhere!' she exclaimed passionately, confident that it would be a 'Bitcoin Killer', and that nobody would ever speak of Bitcoin in the years to come.

By then, the British had already spent almost €30 million on OneCoin. And extravaganzas, like the one at Wembley, only helped increase the rate at which the investors poured money into this strange opportunity.

They'd seen how the renowned success of Bitcoin, a groundbreaking decentralized digital currency, reaped substantial profits for its early backers. And many of those, who could not capitalize on that trend, did not want to miss the bus again.

Between 2014 and 2017, investors from Hong Kong to Pakistan to Canada, and even Palestine, invested over €4 billion in OneCoin.

But in 2017, OneCoin's anxious investors, who failed while desperately trying to convert their coins into cash, attended a gathering at Lisbon, Portugal. They wanted answers and waited for explanations from Ignatova. And guess what?

She never showed up.

Ever since, many international agencies, including the FBI (Federal Bureau of Investigation), have been investigating her whereabouts.

But who is this mysterious woman? And how did she manage to pull off such a legit-looking cryptocurrency scam?

Well, let's take it from the top.

In 2014, Ignatova partnered with Karl Sebastian Greenwood to start a cryptocurrency. They called it OneCoin.

Now you'd think that it would work just like any other cryptocurrency. It would probably have to be mined on a decentralized network of sorts, called a blockchain. For context, a blockchain is a ledger in which every cryptocurrency transaction gets recorded and validated. And it's decentralized because it can run without any oversight or control from a single person, a central authority or even a government.

But with OneCoin, things were different. Investors were just required to enrol for a OneCoin membership, which cost anywhere between €140 and €118,000. The scheme was simple – the bigger the package, the wealthier you'd become. With every membership the investors bought, OneCoin would sell educational course material to them. The courses covered subjects such as cryptocurrencies, trading and investing, and was considered OneCoin's main business.

These memberships also provided tokens to buy OneCoins, which could be converted into cash on an exchange that the company built. The investors could buy expensive Guccis, Lamborghinis, villas or anything else they desired. And since their coins would determine their value from the demand and supply on a blockchain it operated over, more people would mean a stronger OneCoin and richer investors.

It was quite a sparkling 'get rich quick' scheme. And people were getting rich for real, too. But here's what we didn't tell you.

OneCoin's membership packages also lured its investors to sell OneCoins to their friends, family and acquaintances, so that it could build a network and rake in more money.

To put things into perspective, imagine a scenario in which you pay €1000 and buy a OneCoin package. You get access to its courses, and tokens to buy more OneCoins. You then tell two of your friends to buy a package. You tell them how amazing OneCoin's content is and that they can actually buy expensive stuff a few years later with the OneCoins they have.

If you are able to convince them, you earn a cut for hiring new people. The friends carry forward this chain, and the more people all of you have working under you, the more money you make.

If your friends don't want to join the scheme, that works perfectly too. You can still make money by just selling OneCoins.

And for it to seem genuine, OneCoin started off with large multilevel marketing agencies, which already had established networks of people. These agencies would obviously be able to quickly sell more OneCoins and memberships. So it would create the perfect mirage of huge earnings.

One successful multilevel marketer based out of the Netherlands, for instance, was able to make a whopping €90,000 in his first month itself! And many such marketers would be invited to expensive parties and events, like the one Ignatova hosted at Wembley. That's how tactfully OneCoin expanded its network. In fact, it was an apt pyramid scheme.

For OneCoin's investors, it was a flawless money-minting machine backed by an Oxford alumnus, a PhD holder from Konstanz and an ex-employee of McKinsey & Company, a respected management consultancy firm. Yeah, Ignatova had quite an impressive background.

All of it seemed to be working just fine, until one phone call changed everything. A few months after the Wembley's event, Bjorn Bjercke, a blockchain expert, got a rather shocking job offer. The recruitment agent who contacted him offered him a hefty pay package and perks.

His role? To create a blockchain for OneCoin!

Now, you can imagine what a whammy that would be. A cryptocurrency company had been operating for nearly three years without a blockchain!

And that tip off was enough to bring everything down like a house of cards. Bjercke blew the whistle on OneCoin, and soon enough cryptocurrency enthusiasts discovered the truth, finding out that Ignatova and her partners in crime were manually assigning values to OneCoin. That's how its value really exploded. And the course material it sold was mostly plagiarized as well.

Bjercke (and the others who found out the reality) tried to alert OneCoin investors too. But the trust Ignatova had built was hard to break. Several global governments, such as Bulgaria, Finland and Norway, even began cracking down on OneCoin's shenanigans. And in 2016, Hungary's Central Bank warned that OneCoin was a pyramid scheme. But despite these red flags, investors refused to believe that their 'Cryptoqueen' could be a scamster.

They only began to smell something fishy when OneCoin's exchange began to fall apart. See, investors who owned coins could convert their coins into cash whenever they wanted to, on a private exchange called 'xcoinx.com'. OneCoin obviously paid them from the pool of wealth they'd created. It was like paying old investors with new investors' money. That's how pyramid schemes work.

Since this exchange set daily limits on the number of OneCoins the investors could sell, there wasn't a risk of investors withdrawing their money all at once.

But, at the beginning of 2017, OneCoin

abruptly shut down its exchange on the pretext of being under maintenance. Investors couldn't cash out their coins. And weirdly, it never reopened.

The only way investors could know what was really happening was to attend the OneCoin event at Lisbon, where Ignatova would make an appearance. But when that did not take place, it all began to make sense. Ignatova had vanished into thin air, leaving her accomplices in trouble. In 2023, Greenwood was sentenced to twenty years in prison, and was ordered to pay up $300 million.

As for Ignatova, chatter around her plausible death has been doing the rounds since mid-June 2024. Investigations suspect that a Bulgarian drug lord, whom she had hired to protect her, may have actually killed her.

But without real proof, the FBI won't strike her name off their 'Ten Most Wanted Fugitives' list. Could that mean that Ignatova is still alive?

Well, we can't really tell. For all you know, she could be smartly faking her death to divert the attention of investigators, while living her best life on a yacht with the billions she swindled.

WHY ARE INDIAN MALLS DYING?

It's happening.

Malls are dying.

And the ones that are on life support will also likely go under soon. That's according to a real estate consultant firm, Knight Frank.

But before we discuss the sad reality of 'dying malls', let's look at what a successful mall looks like. A good example is the Select Citywalk Mall in Delhi, owned and operated by Select Infrastructure Private Limited, and located in Saket (South Delhi), one of India's wealthiest residential areas. The mall opened to the public in 2007 and boasts a near 100% occupancy rate, with a healthy mix of international (17%) and domestic brands, which are properly zoned and housed across 500,000 square feet of prime leasable area.

It also hosts three anchor stores (stores that pull in people by the masses) – H&M, Zara and Decathlon, alongside a six-screen multiplex, a food court, dedicated zones for fashion and lifestyle, groceries, home and electrical brands, and adequate parking space. And considering that the mall is just a stone's throw away from the metro station, it's no wonder that this urban consumption centre has generated the highest sales per square foot and the highest footfall in the country among any Indian mall of comparable size.

This is what success looks like.

But there is also another kind of mall. One that's barely occupied. There are no anchor stores, no movie screens, no food courts, no people. There may be a few spas and a liquor store, but with hardly any customers flocking to the stores. It feels eerie, with parts of the mall so decrepit you could mistake it for a haunted house.

So the real question is: How does a mall go from being a bustling centre of human activity and commerce to a ghostly shell?

Well, you would think that ghost malls emerge when there's a general decline of human activity in the area surrounding the mall. Or you may believe the mall loses its sheen when people lose interest. However, that's only partly true. A good chunk of malls go bust because of bad management.

Take, for instance, the case of the Grand Venice Mall. As an article in the *Print* notes: It once featured 'Roman statues, domes, Venetian-styled architecture, and louvred windows… two canals running under its arches, with gondola rides on offer so that visitors can get a Venice-like experience in Uttar Pradesh. However, the mall and its reputation began to deteriorate after the Economic Offences Wing (EOW) of the Delhi police arrested the mall's owner Satinder Singh Bhasin in 2020 for his alleged role in the ₹4,000 crore Bike Bot scam.'

> **Sidebar:** 'The Bike Bot scam was a scheme that promised customers large returns on their investment in motorcycles that were supposed to be used as two-wheeler taxis.'

Once the mall owner is implicated, management and upkeep take a back seat. Soon enough, the anchor stores walk away. This takes away a good chunk of the crowd, and the reduced footfall in turn affects everyone that's left. If you don't have enough retail stores, it affects footfall again. It's a vicious, never-ending cycle. In fact, in its report on ghost malls, Knight Frank writes that vacancy rates in Grade C stock (small, bad malls) have gone up even when Grade A shopping centres' operational metrics continue to improve.

That's the point. Not all malls are dying. But the ones that are doing poorly are most likely doomed.

And it doesn't always happen because the mall owner goes bankrupt, or he is implicated in a 'Bike Bot scam'. Sometimes it could happen because of short-term incentives. As a mall developer, you want to make sure that you break even on your investment as quickly as possible. And in a rush to lease out spaces, many smaller developers will refuse to strategically allocate retail units. You'll see a random mix of shops. For instance, a food outlet next to a designer apparel store. There are no zones, no clear demarcations.

Sometimes, the developers also divide retail spaces into smaller units, just to push a sale. In the short term this makes money, easing the pressure on an already stressed balance sheet (Yes, real estate developers are constantly short on funds.). But in the long term, it is a terrible strategy, especially if you are looking to attract premium/quality tenants.

And you know what's worse?

Some mall owners don't even care about this. Once they break even on a project, they move on to the next best thing. The funds dedicated to maintenance and upkeep come from the common area maintenance charge, a fee every tenant is expected to pay. If this money doesn't cover the costs, or worse, there's little provision to ramp up this charge, then the mall is doomed. The developer walks away. Larger stores (that can cut their losses soon) also head for the exit, leaving behind a half-empty mall with small business owners who may not have the leverage or the money to switch.

This is how most malls die in India. And it's a terrible sight.

So what happens then?

Well sometimes, a mall owner may really want to breathe new life into the mall. In which case, they'll have to undo some of the damage and also invest some money to re-zone, reprioritize and plan how to attract bigger, better brands – especially in the wake of e-commerce players vying for the same customers. But in cases where there's not much hope of any financial gain, the best option is to let it go. The mall could instead be repurposed into an office space, or torn down to build something else.

And finally, maybe, just maybe, this is the natural order of things. Eventually the ride has to end. A mall has to die. Slow decay until your favourite spot becomes a ghost mall. The only thing that will remain are the memories—of a place that once used to be truly special.

Okay, that was probably a bit cheesy. But you get it.

DO ATMs NEED A PAY RISE?

1.31 lakh.

That's the number of off-site ATMs (automated teller machines) India had at the end of FY23. We're talking about those standalone ATMs that aren't inside a bank's branch. And this figure is about 1.5% more than last year's.

But this tiny growth isn't driven by banks. Their off-site ATMs in fact, have actually dropped by 2% during the same period. So the credit for the increasing trend goes to the White Label ATM Operators (WLAOs). These folks are private ATM service providers like Tata Communication Payment Solutions' Indicash and India1 Payments. Customers from any bank can use them to transact money.

A decade ago, however, things were different. Only public, private or foreign banks could set up and operate ATMs. But the high-cost infrastructure ate into their profitability. The banks had to pay rent for ATM spaces, employ security systems and personnel, and refill ATMs with cash. The capital or one-time costs of owning ATMs added up, too. It was an expensive affair.

> **Sidebar:** ATMs operated by Scheduled Commercial Banks (public, private, foreign, small finance banks and payment banks) are called brown-label ATMs.

That's probably why banks reduced the deployment of ATMs, especially in remote areas where people didn't use debit cards much. This meant that financial inclusion was under threat.

So the RBI had an idea. It said, 'Hey, let's allow the private folks to hop into the ATM business.

They can do all the heavy lifting and incur most of the capital and operational costs. They can expand into rural areas too, while banks can concentrate on their core business. And that way, more and more people can have access to banking at their fingertips.'

That's how WLAOs entered the space in 2012.

But while the number of ATMs is growing, even if at a snail's pace, the number of players in the segment has halved ever since. The ones that are left are demanding a pay rise.

What does this mean?

You see, WLAOs make money mainly through interchange fees. Think of it as the fee that your bank pays another bank or a WLAO when you swipe your card at another bank's ATM or a white-label ATM.

Now, here's the problem. The first three to five swipes are free for customers at any bank's ATM. And the WLAOs start making money only after the cardholders cross this threshold. But the fees they get are quite low.

For instance, in 2012 a WLAO made ₹15

on every financial transaction a customer made at its ATM. In 2021, this went up to ₹17. On the flip side, a 2019 RBI report suggested that the WLAOs had to shell out about ₹60,000 per month to keep an ATM running. So, if they wanted to run profitable businesses, they had to earn at least ₹20 per transaction (including non-financial transactions).

Of course, this is not their only source of revenue. They can earn extra money by displaying advertisements too. But, their expansion into semi-urban and rural spaces isn't working out as expected, because they aren't making enough money to cover the costs, which have been rising over the last few years.

See, since the last interchange fee hike in 2021, the RBI has increased interest rates by 2.5% to keep inflation under control, which simply acts as a disincentive for people and businesses to borrow money. But the cash that WLAOs reload into their ATMs is actually part of their working capital or the money that they need to operate every day. So if they rely on working capital loans, it simply means that the cost of loading cash would climb uphill. Add to that the fact that rentals and fuel costs have been on the rise, and you'll see how things have simply gone for a toss.

Also, the push to change how ATMs are reloaded can increase the near-term costs even further.

See, at the moment, the money is loaded by personnel, who carry sacks of cash with them. During the process, the sacks are placed out in the open, which explains the strict security around this exercise.

The RBI has been trying to make this more secure. It wants to implement a contactless cassette-swapping system. That way, the personnel who reload the cash into these machines would simply have to swap old currency cassettes for new ones, which are locked. They don't even have to touch the money and these cassettes have embedded chips that can count how many notes they contain.

But the thing is that the cost of each cassette could be nearly ₹15,000, and procuring these in large quantities would mean bearing additional costs, which explains why ATM operators have been nudging the RBI to hike interchange fees.

But guess what?

ATM operators can bring down the costs through other means too.

You see, nearly 70% of the 2,60,000 (on-site and off-site) ATMs, including those operated by banks, have machines that have only one practical function – to dispense cash. This makes cash replenishing an expensive proposition. But, if ATM operators set up machines that can accept deposits too, it can recycle that money for cash withdrawals. And this will reduce the number of trips the ATM operators need to make to reload their ATMs.

If you think beyond it, you'll see that footfall at the banks will go down, helping them focus on operations other than time-consuming cash withdrawals and deposits.

So, while the initial costs might be higher, it could be a worthwhile proposition in the long term.

Also, there might be a way to get borrowing costs down for some of these ATM operators.

Look, an RBI report from 2020 pointed out that WLAOs typically access working capital loans from banks at MCLR (Marginal Cost of Funds-based Lending Rate)-linked rates, or the rate below which banks can't lend. And although these rates are linked to the repo rate (the rate at which the RBI lends money to commercial banks), the former is much higher.

To put things into perspective, as of March 2024, the average MCLR is upwards of 8.5%. But the repo rate is lower, at 6.5%.

So, the RBI committee had suggested that letting WLAOs borrow at repo rates rather than MCLR can actually help reduce the operating costs of the WLAOs.

But it doesn't look like the suggestion has been put into practice yet.

So yeah, there seems to be some interesting action taking place in the boring old world of ATMs. We'll have to wait and see what happens next.

REFERENCES

Is this India's decade?

1. **And Borge Brende ...** 'India Witnessing "Snowball Effect", Set to See Exponential Growth in Coming Years: WEF President Borge Brende', *The Hindu*, 26 May 2023, tinyurl.com/mrywzrud.
2. **McKinsey's CEO Bob Sternfels ...** 'It's Not India's Decade, It's India's Century: McKinsey's Sternfels', *Outlook Business & Money*, 2 September 2022, tinyurl.com/ffsdfudd.
3. **Morgan Stanley estimates ...** Ahya, Chetan. 'India's Coming Decade of Outperformance', *Financial Times*, 8 November 2022, tinyurl.com/55a8ewuz.
4. **Nearly 70% of the population falls ...** Bhargava, Yuthika. 'India's GDP Can Grow to $40 Trillion If Working-Age Population Gets Employment: CII Report', *The Hindu*, 3 April 2022, tinyurl.com/ye28hb49.
5. **That's a figure that The Economist called ...** 'India Is Getting an Eye-Wateringly Big Transport Upgrade', *The Economist*, 13 March 2023, tinyurl.com/5bv678u8.
6. **You see, back in 2012 ...** 'Losing Sleep over Subsidy Leakage, Not Subsidy Itself: Pranab Mukherjee', *NDTV Profit*, 19 February 2012, tinyurl.com/zxv49hem.

7. **And apparently, we've saved ...** 'Digital India Ecosystem Plugged $27 Bn in Subsidy Leakage: Ajay Seth, Secretary', ETGovernment.com, 7 March 2023, tinyurl.com/ye244jst.
8. **Foreign companies like Apple ...** Phartiyal, Sankalp. 'Apple Triples India iPhone Output to $7 Billion in China Shift', Bloomberg, 13 April 2023, tinyurl.com/2t25xmez.
9. **There are other things ...** Samuelson, Kate. 'India's Last Village Goes Electric, but Millions Still See Dim Returns', *TIME*, 3 May 2018, tinyurl.com/465m8zwm.
10. **There are other things ...** 'India Is Getting an Eye-Wateringly Big Transport Upgrade', *The Economist*, 13 March 2023, tinyurl.com/5bv678u8.
11. **And that has been something of a struggle ...** 'Educated and Unemployed: India's Angry Young Voters', *The Economic Times*, 12 April 2024, tinyurl.com/mrxyjsu2.
12. **In fact, the government thinks ...** 'India Needs $1.5 Trillion for Infrastructure: Jaitley', *The Hindu*, 26 June 2016, tinyurl.com/2x66nakc.
13. **There's also the matter ...** 'FDI Equity Inflows Dip 22% to $46 Bn in 2022-23', Moneycontrol, 29 May 2023, tinyurl.com/7e2u2uwy.
14. **They've asked companies to ...** Upasani, Siddharth. 'What's Stopping You from Investing? FM Sitharaman Asks India Inc', Moneycontrol, 13 September 2022, tinyurl.com/ycy5c9vj.
15. **And finally, our growth is driven by ...** Garg, Ajay, and Anitha Rangan. 'Role of India's Consumption in Its Growth Story', *The Times of India*, 20 December 2022, tinyurl.com/3248epw7.

Is India getting rid of poverty?

1. **That's how many people ...** Haq, Zia. 'In 9 Years, 248MN Pulled out of Multidimensional Poverty: Niti Aayog Paper', *Hindustan Times*, 16 January 2024, tinyurl.com/mvknpnap.
2. **Yup, the first real measure ...** 'How to Measure Poverty', *The Economist*, 6 April 2023, tinyurl.com/2z34swrt.
3. **For instance, back in the day ...** M., Manjula, and Amalendu Jyotishi. 'For India to Measure Poverty and Achieve Development Goals, It Needs a Multipronged Approach', Scroll.in, 3 March 2022, tinyurl.com/22ydvr74.
4. **For instance, the World Bank pointed out ...** 'Multidimensional Poverty Measure', World Bank Group, 2022, tinyurl.com/2hxf6k6x.
5. **But until then ...** Ranade, Ajit. 'Multidimensional Poverty Data Reopens a Great Debate', *Mint*, 17 January 2024, tinyurl.com/43nsnfzx.

How will India's demographic dividend pan out?

1. **We have overtaken China ...** 'India Population (2024)', Worldometer, 2024, tinyurl.com/7a2z6m57.
2. **Because irrespective of whether ...** 'India@100: Reaping the Demographic Dividend', EY India, 11 April 2023, tinyurl.com/saj74dem.
3. **For instance, Japan in the 1960s ...** Thakur, Atul. 'India Enters 37-Year Period of Demographic Dividend', *The Economic Times*, 22 July 2019, tinyurl.com/28dypazb.
4. **Well, according to a study ...** 'India Skills Report 2024', Wheebox, 2024, https://tinyurl.com/4pfw9pk8.

5. **Sample this from …** Nigam, Neeti. 'The Rise and Fall of the Indian Engineering Degree', *The Indian Express*, 15 January 2020, tinyurl.com/272xrma5.
6. **Also, only 5% of our workforce …** 'How Apprenticeships Can Be a Game-Changer for Skill-Building | Explained', *India Today*, 18 June 2024, tinyurl.com/3m7drvyz.
7. **But for a long time …** Chandra, Jagriti. 'Share of Education in Budgetary Allocations Has Fallen over Last 7 Years', *The Hindu*, 31 January 2023, tinyurl.com/mr3kvhy2.
8. **The International Labour Organization …** 'Educated and Unemployed: India's Angry Young Voters', *The Economic Times*, 12 April 2024, tinyurl.com/mrxyjsu2.
9. **The Pew Survey says …** M.K., Venu. 'Does India Overtaking China in Population Call for a Party?', The Wire, tinyurl.com/7xc243hw.
10. **And creating 93 million jobs …** Joshi, Manoj. 'Crunching the Numbers', Observer Research Foundation, 26 April 2023, tinyurl.com/yyvphrrx.
11. **There's actually a very important …** 'India Starts Survey to Assess Women Participation in Workforce', *The Hindu*, 30 January 2024, tinyurl.com/39c6c828.
12. **But even then …** Singh, Aditi. 'Women Contribute Only 18% to GDP despite 48% Share in Population: Study', *The Economic Times*, 2 March 2024, tinyurl.com/23sdz6af.

Why do the rich keep getting richer?

1. **Take a look at these numbers …** Bharti, Nitin Kumar, et al. 'Income and Wealth Inequality in India, 1922-2023: The Rise of the Billionaire Raj', World Inequality Lab, 2024, tinyurl.com/msynbcva.

2. **So if r ...** Mankiw, N. Gregory. 'Yes, R > G. So What?', *American Economic Review*, Vol. 105, No. 5, May 2015, pp. 43–47, https://tinyurl.com/mtj5vjwx.
3. **As Swaminathan Aiyar ...** Aiyar, Swaminathan S. Anklesaria. 'Piketty's Botched Analysis of Inequality in India', Cato Institute, 16 November 2017, tinyurl.com/yn6vecp4.
4. **In fact, as an article ...** Naím, Moisés. 'The Problem with Piketty's Inequality Formula', *The Atlantic*, 27 May 2014, tinyurl.com/2rcur6dd.

Should we have a four-day workweek?

1. **They even had a slogan ...** 'Industrialization and the Working Class', Digital History, 2021, tinyurl.com/yse9ma98.
2. **But it took a decision ...** 'Ford Factory Workers Get 40-Hour Week', HISTORY, A&E Television Networks, 13 November 2009, tinyurl.com/mpjfmbha.
3. **The Great Depression ...** Sawyer, Kathy. '200 Years Ago - the 12-Hour Day, the 6-Day Week', *The Washington Post*, 24 December 1977, tinyurl.com/359sz3pn.
4. **For instance, Microsoft trialled it out ...** Paul, Kari. 'Microsoft Japan Tested a Four-Day Work Week and Productivity Jumped by 40%', *The Guardian*, 4 November 2019, tinyurl.com/2ypbnetp.
5. **In the UK ...** Laker, Ben, and Thomas Roulet. 'Will the 4-Day Workweek Take Hold in Europe?', *Harvard Business Review*, 5 August 2019, tinyurl.com/yeeytuca.
6. **Well, let's look at the case ...** Pinsker, Joe. 'Kill the 5-Day Workweek', *The Atlantic*, 17 June 2021, tinyurl.com/bde47tx3.

7. **The Economist plotted the hours** ... C.W. 'Proof That You Should Get a Life', *The Economist*, 9 December 2014, tinyurl.com/yck8svdy.
8. **Historian Benjamin Hunnicutt has a theory** ... Pinsker, Joe. 'Kill the 5-Day Workweek', *The Atlantic*, 17 June 2021, tinyurl.com/bde47tx3.

What is the impact of the third gender on the economy?

1. **In fact, nearly 6 in 10** ... Raman, Shreya. 'Denied Visibility in Official Data, Transgender Indians Can't Access Benefits, Services', IndiaSpend, 11 June 2021, tinyurl.com/veka7mas.
2. **A National Human Rights Commissions Survey** ... 'Transgender and Unemployment in India', *Outlook*, 16 February 2022, tinyurl.com/ysxsndt9.
3. **And a few years ago** ... Raman, Shreya. 'Transgenders Can't Get State Benefits as Most Official Data Ignores "Other"', *Business Standard*, 11 June 2021, tinyurl.com/jpm68b34.
4. **In 2020, as India locked down** ... Ibid.
5. **According to data from** ... 'National Portal for Transgender Persons: Ministry of Social Justice and Empowerment - Government of India', transgender.dosje.gov.in, tinyurl.com/3pyey7my.
6. **One report indicates that** ... 'In India, a Private Company Has Come up with a "Manifesto" to Spur Corporations into Implementing Transgender-Friendly Policies', Business Insider, 24 December 2018, tinyurl.com/5x8j53e8.

Were 1991's economic reforms genius – yes or no?

1. **In fact, GDP growth slowed ...** Gupta, Poonam, and Florian Blum. 'India's Remarkably Robust and Resilient Growth Story', World Bank Blogs, The World Bank, 12 April 2018, tinyurl.com/2hyxzmct.
2. **While other developing countries ...** Kim, Kwan S. 'The Korean Miracle (1962-1980) Revisited: Myths and Realities in Strategy and Development', Kellogg Institute for International Studies, November 1991, tinyurl.com/mwstxhe2.
3. **India also went on a ...** Mital, Ankit. 'India and Liberalization: There Was a 1966 before 1991', *Mint*, 24 January 2016, tinyurl.com/v7hy9xse.
4. **In fact, our share of global trade ...** Aiyar, Swaminathan S. Anklesaria. 'Twenty-Five Years of Indian Economic Reform', Cato Institute, 26 October 2016, tinyurl.com/4xmf4uky.
5. **Our external debt ...** Cerra, Valerie, and Sweta Chaman Saxena. 'What Caused the 1991 Currency Crisis in India?', International Monetary Fund, October 2000, https://tinyurl.com/2ba5sp7j.
6. **Well, we had a boatload of gold ...** Khanna, Sundeep. 'Backstory: The Forex Crisis of 1991 and the Pledging of Indian Gold', CNBC-TV18, 21 February 2022, tinyurl.com/2kmppw52.
7. **When PV Narasimha Rao ...** 'On This Day in 1991: A Landmark Budget That Changed India's Fortunes', *The Economic Times*, 24 July 2022, tinyurl.com/ycxeyvs2.
8. **Well, these were Dr Manmohan Singh's final words ...** Singh, Manmohan. 'Budget 1991-92 Speech', 24 July 1991, tinyurl.com/ympn5fb7.

9. **The Foreign Direct Investment ...** Dutta, M. K., and Gopal Kumar Sarma. 'Foreign Direct Investment in India since 1991: Trends, Challenges and Prospects', SSRN, 1 January 2008, http://dx.doi.org/10.2139/ssrn.1443577.
10. **India delivered a 'miracle' ...** 'India GDP Growth Rate 1960–2024', Macrotrends LLC, tinyurl.com/5n7jd4yd.
11. **And between 1990 and 2013 ...** Bhattacharya, Ananya. 'India's Pulled at Least 170 Million People Out of Poverty Since 1990', Quartz, 12 September 2018, tinyurl.com/v9judwvt.
12. **Well, there's no doubt ...** Mital, Ankit. 'India's Industrial Reforms of 1991: The Inside Story', *Mint*, 6 August 2016, tinyurl.com/4rbcs65t.

Should India print more currency if we need money?

1. **As of April 2024 ...** 'Public Debt of the U.S. By Month, 2019–2020', Statista, 15 July 2024, tinyurl.com/yx6d6w7d.

What if we abolished the Income Tax?

1. **In fact, all evidence ...** Gale, William G. 'Don't Buy the Sales Tax', Brookings, 1 March 1998, tinyurl.com/ywt9sv94.
2. **For instance, one idea ...** Amadeo, Kimberly. 'Fair Tax Plan: Pros, Cons, and Effects', The Balance, 31 March 2023, tinyurl.com/cd79jd28.

What is inheritance tax? Is it a good idea?

1. **That's Sam Pitroda's take ...** 'Who Is Sam Pitroda and How His Controversial Remarks Have Put Congress in Soup', Moneycontrol, 26 April 2024, tinyurl.com/bdhkh3t8.
2. **And as of 2021 ...** 'Inheritance Taxation in OECD Countries', The Organization for Economic Cooperation and Development, 2021, https://tinyurl.com/yjprv5un.
3. **A 1993 study called ...** Holtz-Eakin, D., et al. 'The Carnegie Conjecture: Some Empirical Evidence', *The Quarterly Journal of Economics*, Vol. 108, No. 2, May 1993, pp. 413–35, https://doi.org/10.2307/2118337.
4. **But another 2018 study ...** Kinderman, Fabian, Lukas Mayr and Dominik Sachs. 'Inheritance Taxation and Wealth Effects on the Labor Supply of Heirs', National Bureau of Economic Research, September 2018, https://tinyurl.com/2tn9w999.
5. **These basic arguments are probably why ...** Singh, Surbhi Gloria. 'Explained: What the Raging Debate About Inheritance Tax Is All About', *Business Standard*, 26 April 2024, tinyurl.com/5x6tsvve.
6. **In fact, we did have inheritance tax ...** Kamath, Nikhil. 'A Case for Inheritance Tax', *Forbes India*, Network18, 13 January 2022, tinyurl.com/mvcsabjp.
7. **It could also leave less money ...** 'Sam Pitroda Inheritance Tax Debate: What Is Inheritance Tax in India', *The Economic Times*, 25 April 2024, tinyurl.com/k9x9vhz.
8. **It's also why the US ...** Dore, Kate. 'House Republicans Reintroduce Bill to Repeal "Death Tax"', CNBC, 19 January 2024, tinyurl.com/434yzryv.

What is the impact of long notice periods?

1. **According to Gaurav Chattur** … Chattur, Gaurav. '$6 Billion - the Hidden Cost of 90-Day Notice Period to Companies, Economy', *Business Today*, 25 June 2021, tinyurl.com/mry8dfkz.
2. **The attrition rate has** … Biswas, Sayantani. 'Attrition Rate in India Surged to 20.3% in 2022 from 6% in 2020: Check Driving Factors Here', *Mint*, 26 September 2022, tinyurl.com/5n8dtypb.
3. **The attrition rate has** … 'EY Predicts 9.6% Average Salary Increase for India Inc in 2024; Attrition Decline Nears Pre-Pandemic Levels', EY India, 6 March 2024, tinyurl.com/4saxwth2.
4. **But the end result is that** … 'The $5 Billion Hidden Cost of the 90 Day Notice Period!', Catenon, 22 March 2020, tinyurl.com/bj5r8wae.
5. **The Industrial Disputes Act** … Malaviya, Prashaant, and Anirudh Agarwal. 'Notice Period under the Indian Labour and Employment Law Regime', Ahlawat Associates, 31 May 2023, https://tinyurl.com/mr2ds3b8.
6. **Indian states also have their respective** … Bhattacharya, Dippyaman. 'Notice Period under Various Labour and Employment Laws in India', Samisti Legal, 13 August 2022, tinyurl.com/59j8d47a.
7. **Yes, the US has a short notice period** … Adam, Jamela. 'How Much Notice Should You Give When You Resign?', U.S. News & World Report, 28 June 2023, https://tinyurl.com/2a4k6yae.
8. **Yes, the US has a short notice period** … 'Employment Law Overview USA', L&E Global, 29 August 2023, tinyurl.com/33srxhys.

9. **The UK has a regulation ...** 'Handing in Your Notice', GOV.UK, tinyurl.com/vdm9hv9r.
10. **In case an employer terminates ...** 'Redundancy: Your Rights', GOV.UK, https://tinyurl.com/3kfyw8sm.
11. **Something similar happens in ...** Pawłowska-Szulc, Natalia. 'Everything You Need to Know about Notice Periods', Maxima Consulting, 16 February 2023, tinyurl.com/2d9s37sj.

What if women were paid for daily chores?

1. **$10.8 trillion ...** 'Time to Care', Oxfam America, 19 January 2020, tinyurl.com/yc2w9bks.
2. **So while women in India ...** 'Mind the Gap', Oxfam India, 28 March 2019, https://tinyurl.com/temv3p88.
3. **Well, most people recommend ...** Chakravarty, Arundhati. 'Explained: How to Measure Unpaid Care Work and Address Its Inequalities', *The Indian Express*, 2 May 2021, tinyurl.com/2bbj5m3z.
4. **And if you ask India's courts ...** Biswas, Soutik. 'How India Calculates the Value of Women's Housework', BBC, 24 January 2021, tinyurl.com/mtfsjr8u.
5. **As Indira Hirway a professor of economics ...** Hirway, Indira. 'How to Treat Unpaid Work', *The Hindu*, 21 March 2021, tinyurl.com/5acu8mjw.
6. **In fact, political parties ...** Khaitan, Shreya. 'Should Governments Provide Cash Incentives to Women for Their Unpaid Domestic Work?', Scroll.in, 11 April 2021, tinyurl.com/5bbh9e78.
7. **And while the labour force ...** 'Participation of Women in Workforce', Ministry of Labour and Employment, 8 February 2024, https://tinyurl.com/33dczbwf.

8. **Take Uruguay for instance** ... 'Redistribute Unpaid Work', UN Women, 28 February 2017, https://tinyurl.com/3w6ewec8.
9. **For instance, in Belgium** ... Peteghem, Jan Van and Monique Ramioul. 'New Forms of Employment Voucher-Based Work, Belgium', Research Institute for Work and Society, https://tinyurl.com/54fxfs7h.
10. **Finland, Sweden and Denmark** ... Farvaque, Nicolas. 'Developing Personal and Household Services in the EU: A Focus on Housework Activities', DG Employment, Social Affairs and Social Inclusion, January 2013, https://tinyurl.com/4vrsw3k6.
11. **And it seems to have helped** ... 'Wages for Housework', *The Indian Express*, 20 January 2021, tinyurl.com/4cyj4pu9.
12. **Because as Prabha Kotiswaran** ... Khaitan, Shreya. 'Will Payment for Housework Discourage Women from Paid Work?', IndiaSpend, 7 April 2021, tinyurl.com/mpzpne5m.

Where did India's missing monuments go?

1. **At least that's what the Ministry of Culture** ... A., Divya. 'Archaeological Survey of India Will "Delist" Some "Lost" Monuments. What's Happening, and Why?', *The Indian Express*, 26 March 2024, tinyurl.com/mmvbue3y.
2. **See, India's population has ballooned** ... '1947: India in Numbers – What Was the Country's GDP, Population, Per-Capita Income?', Times Now News, 14 August 2020, tinyurl.com/bbrfe39y.

3. **And a few years ago ...** Kaushik, Narendra. 'Agency Monitoring Airports' Security Faces Staff Crunch', *Mumbai Mirror*, 21 March 2008, tinyurl.com/yc3rwx2y.
4. **Well, one theory comes ...** Lakhani, Somya. 'Street Wise: Barakhamba Road, and a Tomb That Disappeared without a Trace', *The Indian Express*, 15 February 2019, tinyurl.com/yzubx8d6.
5. **And as per the World Tourism Organization ...** 'UNWTO Congress to Discuss the Links between Cultural Heritage and Creative Tourism', UN Tourism, 23 November 2016, tinyurl.com/4cf5xd6p.
6. **For instance, according to a disclosure ...** 'Revenue Generated through Entry Fee for Ticketed Monuments of ASI Has Shown an Increase over Last 3 Years', Ministry of Culture, 18 December 2018, https://tinyurl.com/2xx7mzxu.
7. **Or even innovative ideas ...** 'Taj Mahal Emerges as the Highest Revenue Generating Monument in India', *Outlook*, 25 July 2022, tinyurl.com/26cev6nr.
8. **For instance, the monuments in ...** 'Tamil Nadu's Mamallapuram Beats Taj Mahal in Number of Foreign Visitors', *The Indian Express*, 3 October 2022, tinyurl.com/mrykrvmm.
9. **In 2024 it got a measly ...** 'The Annual Outlay for Ministry of Culture in FY 2023-24 Increased by 12.97% to Rs. 3,399.65 Crore', Ministry of Culture, https://tinyurl.com/5bhwm6ze.
10. **Maybe tweaking the law ...** Nath, Damini, 'Centre Plans to Tweak No-Build Zone around Monuments', *The Hindu*, 6 February 2022, tinyurl.com/23z8crsd.

Why does India have a pension problem?

1. **For starters, some estimates say ...** Chandrasekhar, C. P., and Jayati Ghosh. 'The Withering Trend of Public Employment in India', *The Hindu Business Line*, 29 July 2019, tinyurl.com/2uafzdn9.
2. **In fact, the UN thinks ...** Mukhopadhyay, Sounak. 'India's Life Expectancy to Hit 82!', *Mint*, 9 October 2022, tinyurl.com/5fb4mwux.
3. **They called it the ...** 'The Project OASIS Report', OASIS Foundation, 11 January 2000, https://tinyurl.com/4dh22ya6.
4. **In fact, in 2021, an employee union ...** Singh, Vijaita. 'Bring Back Old Pension Scheme, Central Government Employees Write to Cabinet Secretary', *The Hindu*, 6 November 2022, tinyurl.com/4zbzhm3y.
5. **When the Economic Times crunched ...** Gera, Ishaan. 'Reverting to Old Pension Scheme to Cost States Dear, Hit Spending', *The Economic Times*, 6 March 2023, tinyurl.com/2xbstfps.
6. **They might even save ...** Gera, Ishaan. 'Reverting to Old Pension Scheme to Cost States Dear, Hit Spending', *The Economic Times*, 6 March 2023, tinyurl.com/2xbstfps.
7. **He has said, and we quote ...** 'Reviving Old Pension Scheme a Bankruptcy Recipe: Montek Singh Ahluwalia', *The Times of India*, 8 January 2023, tinyurl.com/yw3ymfaa.

How does the RBI make money?

1. **Yet, it made a profit ...** 'Annual Report', Reserve Bank of India, 30 May 2024, https://tinyurl.com/5fmhrkc2.

2. **Through the simple process ...** 'Understanding Seigniorage', Bank of Canada, 18 June 2022, https://tinyurl.com/yzwudps6.

What is the value of a tree?

1. **There's no point replacing ...** Balaji, Poorna. 'A Tree Cut Is Not the Same as a Tree Planted: Understanding "Quick Fix" Solutions to Development Consequences', *Eartha*, 22 February 2017, tinyurl.com/4k4uurx2.
2. **Also, according to a report ...** Mahapatra, Dhananjay. 'Value of a Tree with 100 Years of Life Left Is Rs 72 Lakh, SC Told', *The Times of India*, 4 Feb. 2021, tinyurl.com/3w8hv4n4.

What is Modern Portfolio Theory?

1. **And when he read about this approach ...** D. Hershey Jr, Robert. 'Harry Markowitz, Nobel-Winning Pioneer of Modern Portfolio Theory, Dies at 95', *The New York Times*, 25 June 2023, tinyurl.com/343cchw5.
2. **Or as Investopedia pithily put it ...** McClure, Ben. 'Modern Portfolio Theory: Why It's Still Hip', Investopedia, 6 July 2023, tinyurl.com/43c5r559.
3. **They said that the theory ...** Wilson, David. 'Harry Markowitz, Father of Modern Portfolio Theory, Dies at 95', Bloomberg, 26 June 2023, tinyurl.com/yckt3kzn.
4. **Four decades later ...** 'Press Release', The Nobel Prize, 16 October 1990, tinyurl.com/y5vvtjsh.
5. **In 2023, Goldman Sachs ...** Mackintosh, James. 'Blackrock vs. Goldman in the Fight over 60/4', *The Wall Street Journal*, 5 January 2023, tinyurl.com/5hd94dh8.

What is the Buffett Indicator? Is it foolproof?

1. **India's stock market capitalization ...** Modak, Samie. 'The Milestone March: India's Market Capitalisation Hits $5 Trillion', *Business Standard*, 21 May 2024, tinyurl.com/pbmn8dvz.
2. **For instance, the number of companies ...** Coutinho, Ashley. 'In a First, BSE M-Cap Tops $5 Trillion; High Valuation a Worry', *The Hindu Business Line*, 21 May 2024, tinyurl.com/39hu843h.
3. **It's at 154% ...** Modak, Samie. 'The Milestone March: India's Market Capitalisation Hits $5 Trillion', *Business Standard*, 21 May 2024, tinyurl.com/pbmn8dvz.
4. **Research by YCharts ...** 'Which Leading Indicators Best Predict Market Declines?', YCharts, 18 July 2022, tinyurl.com/mwx4dat5.
5. **But you could argue ...** Vohra, Navin. 'The Buffett Indicator Revisited: Market Cap-To-GDP and Valuations', Enterprising Investor, CFA Institute, 29 January 2021, tinyurl.com/4nydp6r8.
6. **The Buffett Indicator doesn't ...** 'The Buffett Indicator Suggests That the US Stock Market Is Overvalued', Current Market Valuation, 31 May 2024, tinyurl.com/379nncmx.
7. **The Buffett Indicator was coined ...** Patton, Mike. 'Why Warren Buffett Might Be Wrong', *Forbes*, 30 April 2016, tinyurl.com/24rzkk7d.
8. **But that may not make much sense ...** Krishnan, Aarati. 'The Buffett Indicator Is Not for India', *The Hindu Business Line*, 11 January 2018, https://tinyurl.com/4znsuauf.
9. **In the US, over 58% ...** Caporal, Jack. 'How Many Americans Own Stock? About 145 Million – But the

Wealthiest 10% Own More than 80%', The Motley Fool, 2 November 2021, tinyurl.com/4khsey6j.

10. **In the US, over 58% ...** '17 PC Indian Households Invest in Stocks; Onus on I-Bankers to Get Good Cos to Markets: NSE Chief', *The Economic Times*, 30 October 2023, tinyurl.com/4448dyn7.

Why are TV news stock recommendations a sham?

1. **In it, he wrote: 'The astrological laws ...** Chandra Dutt, Fakir. *Market Forecasting*, Cosmological Economics, 1949.
2. **He wrote: 'The look-out ...** Chandra Dutt, Fakir. *Market Forecasting*, Cosmological Economics, 1949.
3. **In fact, when researchers ...** MS, James Grant CPA. *Avoiding Investment Blunders*. Google Books, Page Publishing Inc., 18 February 2015, tinyurl.com/32j752tc.
4. **In fact, if there's one criticism ...** 'Finception | Simplifying Stock Markets', Finception, tinyurl.com/kne9fsdj.

How can you be a rational investor?

1. **In his seminal essay ...** E. Tetlock, Philip. *Expert Political Judgment: How Good Is It? How Can We Know?*, Princeton University Press, 20 August 2006.

What are tax havens and why do they exist?

1. **According to an article ...** Fitzgibbon, Will, and Ben Hallman. 'What Is a Tax Haven? Offshore Finance,

Explained', International Consortium of Investigative Journalists, 6 April 2020, tinyurl.com/bdeb2ad4.
2. **'Because information can be hard to extract ...** Díaz-Struck, Emilia, and Cecile S. Gallego. 'Beyond Panama: Unlocking the World's Secrecy Jurisdictions', International Consortium of Investigative Journalists, 9 May 2016, tinyurl.com/4wpc6xst.
3. **By some estimates ...** Alstadsæter, Annette, et al. 'Who Owns the Wealth in Tax Havens? Macro Evidence and Implications for Global Inequality', *Journal of Public Economics*, Vol. 162, June 2018, pp. 89–100, https://doi.org/10.1016/j.jpubeco.2018.01.008.
4. **As one report notes ...** Carden, David L. 'To Pay for the Pandemic, Dry Out the Tax Havens', *Foreign Policy*, 16 July 2020, tinyurl.com/y65nyp9r.
5. **For instance, in India ...** 'Interim Budget 2024: What Record Income-Tax Collections Don't Tell You About the Number of Taxpayers', *The Times of India*, 2 February 2024, tinyurl.com/2s39m9ef.
6. **As one report in the BBC notes ...** 'Paradise Papers: The Accident That Led to Britain's Offshore Empire', BBC, 8 November 2017, tinyurl.com/mtpzfyhz.

What are the brands that have helped build India?

1. **Back in the day, parents ...** Misra, Shubhangi, and Samira Sood. 'The Ad That Made Godrej Storwel a Family Essential in the 1970s and '80s', *The Print*, 9 February 2020, tinyurl.com/ffjxab9y.
2. **In the 1980s ...** Guruprasad Gp. '1985-90: Godrej Storwel TV Ads (Godrej Storewell Steel Almirah

Wardrobe)', YouTube, 10 November 2017, tinyurl.com/2cfk6jyb.

3. **According to the then plant manager ...** Jain, Bhavika. 'This Bombay Factory Made Ballot Boxes for India's First Poll', *The Times of India*, 17 March 2019, tinyurl.com/yc4yymp4.

4. *Fun fact ...* 'Godrej Group - the Ballot Box Was a Result of Over 50 Designs by Godrej. The Best Part - Each Finished Ballot Box Cost the States Only Rs. 5. The Interesting Part - If All the Boxes Were to Be Placed Side by Side, They Would Stretch for 200 Miles and If They Were Put on Top of Each Other, They Would Reach the Height of 36 Mount Everest Piled on Top of Each Other!', Godrej Group, Facebook, 2 December 2016, tinyurl.com/2p9mhymu.

5. **But in the 1970s ...** Altstedter, Ari, and Anna Edney. 'Culture of "Bending Rules" in India Challenges U.S. Drug Agency', *The Economic Times*, 31 January 2019, tinyurl.com/3bdakzrz.

6. **Well, you could probably credit ...** 'India at 75: From Ambanis to Bajaj - 20 Doyens Who Shaped India's Business', *Business Standard*, 12 August 2022, tinyurl.com/22tkkehj.

7. **India still upheld ...** Lane, Richard. 'Yusuf Hamied: Leader in the Indian Generic Drug Industry', *Perspectives*, Vol. 386, No. 10011, 12 December 2015, https://doi.org/10.1016/S0140-6736(15)00839-9.

8. **Instead of routing the milk ...** 'How Kuriens Idea Helped India Become World's Largest Milk Producer', Amul, tinyurl.com/376jtk5w.

What is the price of your attention?

1. **'Facebook is free …** Ashley, Michael. 'Sick of the Attention Economy? It's Time to Rebel', *Forbes*, 24 November 2019, tinyurl.com/3cbha9xt.
2. **Red is a trigger colour …** Lewis, Paul. '"Our Minds Can Be Hijacked": The Tech Insiders Who Fear a Smartphone Dystopia', *The Guardian*, 6 October 2017, tinyurl.com/2zu8h6kw.
3. **According to a leaked report …** Levin, Sam. 'Facebook Told Advertisers It Can Identify Teens Feeling "Insecure" and "Worthless"', *The Guardian*, 1 May 2017, tinyurl.com/5hd4mwct.

Why are CEOs overpaid and employees underpaid?

1. **Chief executive officers …** Menon, Asha. 'CEOs Get Paid 130 Times More than a Regular Employee in India Inc: Crisil', Moneycontrol, 27 May 2022, tinyurl.com/yc2dt8tb.
2. **The CEO-to-worker pay gap …** Johnson Hess, Abigail. 'In 2020, Top CEOs Earned 351 Times More than the Typical Worker', CNBC, 15 September 2021, tinyurl.com/3ewu4cdr.
3. **And some studies show …** Anderson, Sarah. 'How the CEO-Worker Pay Gap Deepens Income and Wealth Inequality', Inequality.org, 17 March 2021, tinyurl.com/rvvpd33k.
4. **In fact, some studies show that capping CEO salaries …** Bae, Kee-Hong, et al. 'Restricting CEO Pay Backfires: Evidence from China', *ECGI Working Paper Series in*

Finance, European Corporate Governance Institute, May 2021, tinyurl.com/6vja6bud.
5. **For instance, Alex Edmans ...** Edmans, Alex. 'Why We Need to Stop Obsessing over CEO Pay Ratios', *Harvard Business Review*, 23 February 2017, tinyurl.com/yruhjd8z.

How did businesses forge ahead after Partition?

1. **But a man called ...** Kashyaap, Sindhu. 'How the Swadeshi Movement Led to the Birth of Parle G Biscuits from a Cattle Shed', YourStory, 14 August 2017, tinyurl.com/mryzj448.
2. **And when a biscuit factory ...** Kashyaap, Sindhu. 'How the Swadeshi Movement Led to the Birth of Parle G Biscuits from a Cattle Shed', YourStory, 14 August 2017, tinyurl.com/mryzj448.
3. **Their first wheat biscuit emerged ...** Parle, 'About Us', parleproducts.com, 2020, tinyurl.com/yc4hyy78.
4. **Everything was then being rationed ...** Agarwal, Sapna. 'We Don't Want to Sell Parle: Chauhan', *Mint*, 28 November 2012, tinyurl.com/4b4my9y4.
5. **We were left with just ...** Pratap, Rashmi. 'How Corporate India Dealt with Partition', *The Hindu Business Line*, 11 August 2017, tinyurl.com/46pdnjcy.
6. **And today, Parle sells ...** Malviya, Sagar. 'Parle Crosses $2 Billion in Sales during FY22', *The Economic Times*, 23 November 2022, tinyurl.com/2t7cdnba.
7. **This Swadeshi biscuit has ...** 'The Parle-G Story: The World's Largest-Selling Biscuit Brand with Sales of Rs 8000 Crore; Here's the Mystery Behind Parle-G Girl

Who Was Even Rumored to Be Sudha Murty', *Financial Express*, 30 July 2023, tinyurl.com/4t76xjxt.

8. **Fun fact: If the total number of Parle-G ...** Bhatt, Shephali. 'Parle-G: The Journey of a Biscuit for Masses', *The Economic Times*, 30 October 2013, tinyurl.com/4x8p78pk.

9. **The year was 1906 ...** 'Legacy: When You Feel Like Giving Up, Remember Why You Started', Hamdard, https://tinyurl.com/586bpbdz.

10. **The year was 1906 ...** Mashal, Mujib. 'Across Borders and Divides, One "Heavenly" Refresher Cools Summer Heat', *The New York Times*, 7 July 2021, tinyurl.com/2ax54xf3.

11. **Hakim Majeed's younger son ...** 'Businesses - Global Footprint - Our Presence', Hamdard, https://tinyurl.com/y426hc92.

12. **His elder son Hakim Abdul Majeed ...** 'Indo-Pak Rooh Afza Battle: Delhi HC Permanently Restrains Sale of Pakistani-Owned "Rooh Afza" on Amazon', *The Indian Express*, 15 November 2022, tinyurl.com/4eswfvv5.

13. **In fact, today Rooh Afza accounts ...** Pathak, Sushmita. 'Across South Asia, This Sweet Drink Is Synonymous with Summertime Refreshment', National Public Radio, 5 August 2023, tinyurl.com/bdxbcpea.

14. **Such is the demand ...** 'Rooh Afza Disappears from Market as Ramzaan Fast Begins', *The Economic Times*, 9 May 2019, tinyurl.com/5n7z2rzu.

15. **Such is the demand ...** Singh, Rishika. 'Why Has Delhi HC Asked Amazon to Stop Selling Rooh Afza Made in Pakistan?', *The Indian Express*, 13 Sept. 2022, tinyurl.com/tczk7mj3.

16. **So a Dutch company ...** Susan Pinto, Viveat. '40 Years Ago...And Now: How Dalda Built, and Lost, Its

Monopoly', *Business Standard*, 5 March 2015, tinyurl.com/y2zn3kfc.
17. **By 1956, Unilever had** ... 'HUL History', Hindustan Unilever Limited, tinyurl.com/yp39kpf3.
18. **So, in the 1950s, Unilever** ... 'Who We Are', Dalda, https://tinyurl.com/292nautu.
19. **In India, it sold Dalda to Bunge** ... 'About Us - Dalda Vanaspati', Dalda Vanaspati, tinyurl.com/4zwe9ef5.
20. **In 2023, the Pakistani counterpart** ... Mangi, Faseeh. 'Mega IPO Planned for 2023 by Pakistan's Biggest Cooking Oil Maker', Bloomberg, 23 January 2023, tinyurl.com/yeymyntv.

The biggest crypto scam in history?

1. **'OneCoin is on course to becoming** ... 'Cryptoqueen: How This Woman Scammed the World, Then Vanished', BBC, 24 November 2019, https://tinyurl.com/sjd3j3a9.
2. **Several global governments** ... Roy, Samadrita. 'In Pursuit with John Walsh on ID: What Was the Onecoin Scam All About?', Sportskeeda, 19 June 2024, tinyurl.com/3cpvkfa8.
3. **And in 2016, Hungary's** ... Higgins, Stan. 'Hungary's Central Bank Organizes Task Force against OneCoin', CoinDesk, 10 May 2017, tinyurl.com/u9hmzwrb.
4. **See, investors who owned coins** ... 'United States of Amnerica v. Konstantin Ignatov, Defendant', https://tinyurl.com/wm55fey7.
5. **In 2023, Greenwood was sentenced** ... Thomas, David. 'OneCoin Legal Officer Gets 4 Years in Prison for Crypto Scheme', Reuters, 4 April 2024, tinyurl.com/2eaczsax.

6. **As for Ignatova ...** 'Missing Cryptoqueen Ruja Ignatova's Links to Bulgarian Underworld', BBC, 3 June 2024, tinyurl.com/2p8xrdua.
7. **But without real proof ...** 'Ten Most Wanted Fugitives - RUJA IGNATOVA', Federal Bureau of Investigation, tinyurl.com/mvwd8d3n.

Why are Indian malls dying?

1. **That's according to a real estate ...** Agarwal, Divya, et al. 'Think India Think Retail – 2024', Knight Frank, 2024.
2. **Take, for instance, the case of Grand Venice Mall ...** Bagchi, Dishha, and Gaurvi Narang. 'NCR Has a Graveyard of Ghost Malls — Eerie Storefronts, Broken Mannequins, Mammoth Losses', *ThePrint*, 31 October 2022, tinyurl.com/2mhrttau.

Do ATMs need a pay rise?

1. **1.31 lakh ...** S. Herwadkar, Snehal. *Report on Trend and Progress of Banking in India 2022-23*. Reserve Bank of India, 31 March 2023, https://tinyurl.com/yz6pmu5b.
2. **So the RBI had an idea ...** 'Report of the Committee to Review the ATM Interchange Fee Structure', Reserve Bank of India, 2 October 2019, https://tinyurl.com/hyws6j5d.
3. **But while the number of ATMs is growing ...** Shukla, Piyush. 'White-Label ATMs See Red in Under a Decade', *Financial Express*, 27 June 2023, tinyurl.com/3tsycjyj.
4. **In 2021, this went up to ₹17 ...** Nayak, Gayatri. 'ATM Manufacturers Seek Higher Interchange Rates',

The Economic Times, 20 September 2023, tinyurl.com/2ep3vpsf.

5. **They can earn extra money ...** 'RBI Allows White Label ATM Operators to Source Cash, Generate Income from Ads', *The Hindu Business Line*, 7 March 2019, tinyurl.com/3ycaxktt.
6. **So if they rely on working capital loans ...** Ramanathan, Ajay. 'White-Label ATM Operators Seek Hike in Interchange Fee', *Financial Express*, 31 January 2023, tinyurl.com/3ph83b35.
7. **It wants to implement a contactless ...** Mohan, Raghu. 'ATM Deployers May Get a Boost; Higher Cash Withdrawal May Cost More', *Business Standard*, 28 April 2024, tinyurl.com/5n78skfe.
8. **But the thing is that the cost ...** Nayak, Gayatri. 'ATM Manufacturers Seek Higher Interchange Rates', *The Economic Times*, 20 September 2023, tinyurl.com/2ep3vpsf.
9. **You see, nearly 70% ...** 'Cassette-Swap: Mechanism to Make ATMs Better Will Miss Deadline Again', *Business Standard*, 10 March 2024, tinyurl.com/3k4ak7w7.
10. **But, if ATM operators set up machines ...** Manikandan, Ashwin. 'You Can Soon Deposit Cash at Any ATM', *The Economic Times*, 9 January 2020, tinyurl.com/pr23bdr8.
11. **To put things into perspective ...** Prasad, Ajit. 'Lending and Deposit Rates of Scheduled Commercial Banks – March 2024', Reserve Bank of India, 8 March 2024, tinyurl.com/35jzahm4.

ABOUT FINSHOTS

Finshots is India's most loved financial newsletter, with over 500,000 subscribers and 1.5 million social media followers. Launched in 2019 from a dorm room at IIM-Ahmedabad, Finshots has pursued a clear mission: to build a community that will shape India's financial future.

In just three minutes daily, Finshots simplifies the latest updates in finance, business and the Indian economy – in a language you can easily understand. No fluff, no jargon – just crisp insights. With its signature conversational storytelling, Finshots has democratized financial knowledge for Indian millennials and Gen-Z, making dreaded finance topics fun!